BEYOND BAPTISM

BEYOND BAPTISM

Fannie L. Houck

What the New Believer Should Know About the Adventist Lifestyle

REVIEW AND HERALD PUBLISHING ASSOCIATION
Washington, DC 20039-0555
Hagerstown, MD 21740

The author assumes full responsibility for the accuracy of all facts and quotations as cited in this book.

This book was
Edited by Raymond H. Woolsey
Designed by Richard Steadham
Cover photo by Meylan Thoresen
Type set: 11/12 Palatino

PRINTED IN U.S.A.

Library of Congress Cataloging in Publication Data

Houck, Fannie L., 1933-
Beyond baptism.

Bibliography: p.
1. Seventh-day Adventists. 2. Adventists. I. Title.
BX6154.H59 1987 286.7'32 87-9443

ISBN 0-8280-0377-7

Acknowledgments

The author gratefully acknowledges the contributions of the following who reviewed portions of this manuscript and offered suggestions for improving it: Stoy Proctor, Perry Pedersen, Floyd Bresee, Don E. Crane, and Ron and Karen Flowers. And to Kenneth J. Mittleider, George E. Knowles, and Edward G. (Skip) McClannahan, a special thank-you for timely help and encouragement.

Contents

FIGURES AND TABLES

Figures

Tables

Introduction

Baptism opens the door to membership in the Seventh-day Adventist Church. Beyond it is a new lifestyle. For the new believer, the new way of living has far-reaching effects. This book is prepared so that the new believer can acquaint himself or herself with vocabulary and information essential to growth and witness. Knowing what the total Adventist lifestyle involves can help the new member step into it more quickly and with greater confidence.

It is important that the new believer "settle in" to the Christian way of life quickly and solidly. This process, called discipling, includes learning how to gain spiritual victory, how to prioritize and use personal resources in God's service, and how to work effectively for Him.

Adopted children soon discover how the new family operates and what is expected of them. So, too, in the church. As each new generation of believers becomes oriented and firmly established, they discover what the church is all about. They learn about existing avenues of service and how to achieve optimum health, spiritual growth, and happiness. As traditional Adventist values become their own, they benefit from them.

Before baptism, new believers study the basic doctrines of the Bible. These teachings provide a solid foundation for the new life in Christ. Sabbath-keeping practices stem from belief in the sanctity of the seventh-day Sabbath. Knowing that probation will soon close and

Christ will return gives a sense of urgency and mission to daily life.

Just as important is the parallel study of practical aspects of Christian living—how faith affects lifestyle practices. *Beyond Baptism* describes areas that reveal the Adventist's commitment—Christian service, health, education, stewardship, and response to spiritual counsel in sensitive areas such as personal conduct, dress, diet, and recreation. In attempting to foster Christian maturity in the reader, this book touches on everyday realities and shows how belief can affect daily living.

As should be expected, personal practices vary. However, trends stemming from Adventists' underlying beliefs *do* exist. These traditional Adventist values, based on biblical teachings, are identified so that the new generation of Adventists will be well informed, see their value, and benefit from them.

New members are urged to study this book prayerfully, and adjust their life habits as the Holy Spirit directs. This book is also meaningful for those who have spent a number of years in the church, and it will give practical suggestions on how to answer questions that new believers need answers for.

Beyond Baptism can be a springboard to discussion and exploration.

Kenneth Mittleider
General Vice President
General Conference of Seventh-day Adventists

PART ONE

The Local Church

Gathering Together:

Assemblies and Ceremonies

1 "For where two or three are gathered together in my name, there am I in the midst of them" (Matt. 18:20).

What goes on inside a typical Seventh-day Adventist church on Sabbath? Let's step inside and find out.

Sabbath School

Sabbath school is in session. In the sanctuary the assembled adults sing a hymn and then kneel for prayer. Next someone tells of the needs of a mission school in a foreign nation. Soon the adults gather in groups to discuss the week's Bible lesson. This is the "church at study," using curriculum materials prepared by Bible scholars.

From other rooms of the building comes the sound of children singing. In one room toddlers enjoy a finger play and then place brightly colored felt figures on a flannel board. In another, primary boys and girls listen to stories about nature and missionaries at work. Elsewhere older youth discuss ways they can share their faith in Jesus.

At Bible lesson time, cradle roll children (birth to 3

years) study lessons that repeat yearly. Kindergarten and primary lessons follow a three-year cycle. The church selects the Sabbath school leaders. The Sabbath school council appoints teachers.

Someone mentions one of this quarter's mission projects. Quarter refers to a three-month period of the church year, the quarters being January through March, April through June, July through September, and October through December.

Another person talks about the lesson quarterly, meaning the Bible lesson pamphlets prepared by the world church. These provide study materials for three months and include thought questions and topics for discussion. Some Adventist publishing houses outside North America limit themselves to printing Sabbath school quarterlies in local languages only. At this writing, Sabbath school lessons are published in 108 languages. New lesson quarterlies are given to Sabbath school members at the end of each quarter.

Back in the 1880s the Sabbath school assumed responsibility for raising funds for missions. It still promotes giving to missions. Globally these weekly mission offerings include eggs, sweet potatoes, and other produce, as well as money.

Some Sabbath schools show *Mission Spotlight,* a monthly sound-slide show that helps Adventists see what their mission dollars accomplish. *Mission Spotlight* highlights the area or areas that will benefit from the next Thirteenth Sabbath Offering.

Thirteenth Sabbath Offering. On the thirteenth (or last) Sabbath of each quarter the Sabbath school takes up a special offering. One fourth of it directly benefits that quarter's specified projects. The rest goes into the general world mission budget.

Birthday-Thank Offering. The adult Sabbath school takes up a monthly offering to express gratitude for birthdays and other blessings. This goes to missions, as do children's birthday offerings.

Investment. Investment raises additional funds for missions. Individuals dedicate (invest in) a personal project, asking God to bless it. Investment projects involving saving, sales, and services net more than $4 million a year. Some people save coins, bake and sell bread, or donate a percentage of their commissions.

The Worship Service

After the Sabbath school classes dismiss, the congregation gathers in the sanctuary for the worship service. This includes Scripture reading, congregational singing, prayer, an offering, and a sermon or Bible study. Adventists customarily kneel for prayer, showing reverence for God, in church and Sabbath school.

The assembled congregation may deal briefly with transfers of membership, selection of delegates, or hearing and accepting the nominating committee's report for the selection of church and Sabbath school officers. Church business meetings are held on days other than Sabbath.

Conservative Adventists choose to dress in an appropriate and modest way. Although local customs vary, girls and women most often wear dresses or skirts to church. They use little or no jewelry or colorful cosmetics. Among men, suits and ties tend to predominate, particularly for deacons and elders. The general principles are: be neat, be clean, and dress to honor God.

Camp Meeting

Summer usually brings camp meeting, a yearly spiritual feast geared to the entire church family. The meetings may last for a weekend or for 10 days. Some attendees live in tents or trailers. Others commute.

Camp meeting is a time for spiritual growth, fellowship, and renewal. The speakers often are widely known throughout the denomination. In addition, instruction is offered in subjects such as health, Christian witnessing, Bible study methods, stewardship, and parenting. Camp meeting offers many opportunities to learn about church ministries, doctrine, and progress.

For many, camp meeting is a convenient time to purchase books, Bibles, Christian music, and cases of vegetarian protein foods from the Adventist Book Center.

.The Pathfinder Club

Where there are youth aged 10 to 15, a coed organization known as the Pathfinder Club provides Christian fun, fellowship, and learning. In 1985 there were almost 300,000 Pathfinders in some 13,000 clubs worldwide.

Marching, camping, hiking, studying practical skills, and pursuing hobbies provide Pathfinders many opportunities for self-discovery. Their organized class study leads them year by year from one rank to another, the highest being Master Guide.

At an Investiture service held each spring, Pathfinders receive class tokens, Honor patches, and other awards. Pathfinders attend fairs and camporees sponsored by their regional leaders. Their service projects range from canned food drives at Halloween to Christmas caroling to giving out Vacation Bible School invitations.

Prayer Meeting

Many congregations hold a midweek service. This is a time of singing, study, prayer, and personal testimony. Usually the pastor or an elder conducts this service.

Week of Prayer

The Week of Prayer, held in the autumn, is a time of renewed dedication to the Lord. Beginning at a Sabbath morning worship hour, it continues with nightly meetings in the church or in private homes. A special issue of the *Adventist Review* provides a devotional reading for each day. This special week concludes on the following Sabbath, when the Annual Sacrifice Offering is received. The offering—a suggested day's or week's wages—goes into the World Budget for missions.

Adventist schools conduct one or more Weeks of

Prayer each year, sometimes calling it Week of Spiritual Emphasis. At the high school and college level, a person outside the institution may be invited to speak at the meetings. He or she counsels those who wish help with spiritual problems. Sometimes selected students present the Week of Prayer.

Rites and Ceremonies

Most of the gatherings mentioned so far in this chapter occur on a regular schedule. Others, such as most of the following rites and ceremonies, do not.

Anointing the Sick

The practice of anointing the sick stems from the counsel of James 5:14-16. It is done privately, but believing family members are usually included. The one desiring physical healing requests the elders (local leaders) of the church to come, anoint him or her, and pray for healing. Participants first search their own heart and confess any known sins. Those in charge pray for God's healing hand upon the patient if that be His will and if it would glorify Him. A drop of olive oil is placed with a fingertip onto the forehead of the sick person.

Healing may be immediate or it may be gradual. Sometimes physical healing does not come. Praying for healing without first giving up unhealthful practices is considered presumptuous.

Baby and Child Dedication

This public declaration usually occurs as a scheduled part of a worship service. Parents bring the child forward and declare their intention to raise the child to know and serve the Lord. A prayer of dedication for both the child and parents follows.

Baptism

Baptism by immersion symbolizes the death of the old, sinful nature and a rebirth in Christ. It recalls His death, burial, and resurrection. Baptism publicly declares the candidate's faith in Christ and desire to live a new life in Him. Immersion baptism is a condition of membership in the Adventist Church.

Those who seek baptism first study thoroughly the church's fundamental beliefs and related issues. When ready, they may be publicly questioned regarding their agreement with the church's major teachings. The congregation then votes them into church membership, effective upon baptism. Though usually conducted in heated water in an indoor tank during a regular worship service, baptisms are sometimes held outdoors.

Wearing long robes, baptismal candidates and the officiating minister step into the water. The minister baptizes them "in the name of the Father, and of the Son, and of the Holy Ghost." The candidate grips the minister's arm and is immersed briefly. After the baptism, the church family often extends the "right hand of fellowship" (handshakes and greetings). Each new member receives a certificate of baptism.

Persons previously baptized by immersion in another denomination sometimes join the church on profession of faith. As a rule children are not baptized before the age of 10 or 12.

When members move to another area or expect to be away from the home church for more than six months, they are encouraged to transfer their membership. Students away at school are an exception.

The member initiates the transfer of membership by asking the clerk of the congregation he is newly attending to send for a letter of membership transfer. After this is done, the home church's board considers the request and seeks the congregation's approval. If the request is approved, the recommendation is sent to the new church; then that church board considers the transfer and presents it to the congregation, where the request is read publicly before a vote is taken.

Communion

A symbolic meal held every three months, the Communion service, or Lord's Supper, commemorates Christ's death on the cross. Self-examination followed by repentance and confession of known sin prepares the participants for this service. Deaconesses prepare the Communion symbols and place them on a table at the front of the sanctuary. These emblems, whole wheat crackers and unfermented grape juice, symbolize the broken body and spilled blood of Christ. Within certain frames of reference, yeast represents sin; therefore for this occasion the bread is unleavened.

The ordinance of humility (foot washing) takes place before the emblems are served. Men and women separate and go to different rooms. In pairs, they wash each other's feet, much as Jesus washed His disciples' feet before the Last Supper. The congregation then reassembles for the serving of the Communion symbols.

Since Adventists practice open Communion, all Christians may participate. Unbaptized children are observers only.

Ordination of Deacons and Elders

Before beginning to serve, deacons and local elders are publicly ordained during a regular worship service. The pastor admonishes them to be faithful in each duty and to set a worthy example of service and piety. Then the pastor and previously ordained local elders kneel around the candidate or candidates. As the pastor prays, these leaders place their hands on the candidates' heads, setting them apart to serve the local congregation.

Ordained deacons and elders who remain members in good standing need not be re-ordained if later voted into the same office in another congregation.

Ordination to the Gospel Ministry

Pastors are ordained by the president of the local conference or some other ministerial leader. This ordination to the gospel ministry takes place at a separate service. It includes the laying on of hands and an ordination prayer. To qualify for ordination, potential ministers generally serve a term of internship during which they demonstrate their call to the ministry. Shortly before the ordination an examination of the candidate reveals the individual's personal religious experience, attitudes, beliefs, and fitness to serve as an ordained minister.

Ordained ministers have authority to baptize, perform marriages, and conduct the Communion service.

What is the purpose of the assemblies and ceremonies outlined in this chapter? In brief, to bring the body of believers closer to God and one another.

PART TWO

At Work Around the World: Christian Service

The Seventh-day Adventist Church operates a wide spectrum of Christian ministries. These require a variety of skilled workers. Adventist missionaries—pastors, nurses, physicians, dentists, technicians, evangelists, administrators, teachers, and others—serve in far-flung parts of the world.

Three words sum up their practical Christian service—people helping people.

From Malamulo to Seoul:

Missions

2 "Go ye therefore, and teach all nations, baptizing them in the name of the Father, and of the Son, and of the Holy Ghost: teaching them to observe all things whatsoever I have commanded you: and, lo, I am with you alway, even unto the end of the world" (Matt. 28:19, 20).

Before commanding His disciples to evangelize the

world, Jesus showed them how by teaching, preaching, and healing.

Although the work of evangelism is unfinished, world conditions signal the nearness of Christ's second coming. Adventists believe they must help take the gospel to the far corners of the world.

Organized in 1863, the Seventh-day Adventist Church sent out its first foreign missionary in 1874.

Missionaries cross sociological, cultural, political, and language barriers. In less-developed nations Adventist missionary work appropriately begins by meeting local needs. The health and educational work at Malamulo in Malawi, Africa illustrates this.

Malamulo, Malawi

Malamulo College, a coeducational boarding school in Africa, currently offers a complete secondary program plus a teacher-training course. Located some 40 miles south of Blantyre, Malawi, it shares 150 acres with Malamulo Hospital and Leprosarium.

An Adventist elementary school opened on property purchased here in 1902. As it grew and developed, the school added classes for girls (1910), teacher training (1925), and a two-year ministerial course (1947). Long known as Malamulo Mission Training Institute, it became Malamulo College in 1963.

Malamulo's medical facility, Malamulo Hospital and Leprosarium, trains nurses and offers full medical care. The leprosarium is half a mile from the main clinical block.

Beginning with a clinic in 1915, the medical work at Malamulo had no permanent hospital buildings until 1927. Responding to local needs, the hospital added treatment of European patients (1929), weekly classes for mothers (1942), a ward for Asians (1942), and a flying-doctor service (1962). A three-year course for African hospital assistants became a four-year program (1954). The government accredited it in 1963. A new four-year course giving girls three years of nursing and one year of midwifery training opened in 1963. There is also a school for laboratory technicians.

Malamulo Hospital now reaches beyond the immediate community with projects such as an outclinic where a medical assistant gives vaccinations and screens young children for abnormalities.

Leper treatment began in 1926. In time the leprosarium accommodated 300 inpatients and 250 outpatients. Since 1973 lepers have been sought out and treated at centers near their home villages instead of at the hospital. The leprosarium is being phased out.

Seoul, Korea

With variations, the story is repeated around the globe. Seventh-day Adventist work in Korea began in 1904. The work developed and expanded. In 1912 a church, publishing house, and mission offices were built near Seoul. A ministerial course began for older students in 1917. The main educational institution developed until it became a liberal arts college (1966) offering, among other subjects, home economics and agriculture (added in 1966), and an English major (added in 1967). At present the school, Korean Sahmyook University, is a coeducational collegiate institution and shares its campus with Korean Union College Academy (high school).

Ministries added later include a Bible correspondence school (1948), radiobroadcasts (1957), English language schools, and a center for U.S. military personnel.

Medical work in Seoul began in two rented rooms downtown (1931). By 1936 the newly built Seoul Sanitarium and Hospital began accepting patients and had opened a school of nursing. By 1986 the 406-bed Seoul Adventist Hospital served a rapidly-expanding city of 9 million. Hospital physicians and nurses regularly conduct charity clinics in villages, as well as health education programs in and around the city.

An orphanage (established 1951) cared for orphans suffering from tuberculosis, malnutrition, and other problems. Some 800 orphans found adoptive homes in the United States or Europe. The government now meets orphans' needs, and this orphanage no longer operates.

The Missionaries

Missionaries voluntarily leave their home country to work in another, putting in long hours for modest wages. Willingly they devote their lives to Christian service, working with diligence and purpose. As some say, "The salary is low but the retirement benefits are 'out of this world.' "

Selection of Missionaries. It is said that all missionaries must be able to do three things—adapt, adapt, and adapt. Innovativeness and flexibility are prime assets. Many missionaries must cope with primitive facilities, inadequate equipment, and/or a shortage of supplies. Others, living in modern homes and cities, face other frustrations. Their highest priority might be an understanding of interpersonal relationships.

The Secretariat of the General Conference (Adventist world headquarters organization) screens, selects, and licenses candidates for mission service. It arranges transportation and, when needed, language study and instruction in tropical medicine. Each year many new missionaries are sent out and others return to their posts after a brief furlough in their homeland.

Other Missionaries. In the student missionary program, baptized Adventist youths between the ages of 18 and 30 volunteer for a year of mission service, taking time from college or work. In many cases they pay their way to and from an established mission post. There they work alongside full-fledged missionaries, often teaching English to adults. Usually the student missionaries do not need to learn a foreign language. They receive room and board plus a small monthly stipend for personal expenses.

Retired denominational employees also volunteer for one- to two-year terms as missionaries in a program called Special Overseas Service (SOS). While duties vary, they have included teaching accounting and English composition.

Financial Support. Through appropriations at the General Conference (GC) level, the church provides substantial portions of many mission budgets. These funds cover items such as the salaries of missionaries. This financial base stabilizes the church's missions. Missionaries do not depend upon a few specific congregations or individuals at home for their support.

Missionary work outside North America involves, among other things, high schools and colleges, English language schools, evangelistic complexes, hospitals and sanitariums, dispensaries and clinics, airplanes for reaching remote areas, orphanages and retirement homes, publishing houses, radio/TV production centers, and Bible correspondence schools.

The Results

Although Christian missions promote proper diet and better health and offer practical help, their main purpose is to win people to Christ. Church growth follows.

Workers trained in Adventist schools around the world take up the evangelistic, educational, and medical work in their own and other countries. A century ago the majority of Adventists lived in the United States. These people largely financed as well as staffed the foreign missions. In recent years this picture has changed. Now well-educated missionaries from Europe, Australia, the Philippines, and other countries also serve in other nations.

In places such as Mexico City, rapid church growth has resulted from the combined work of pastors, churches, schools, physicians, health classes, Bible correspondence courses, and evangelistic campaigns.

Staying Welcome Abroad. Believing in the separation of church and state, the Adventist Church has adopted a nonpolitical stance. This allows the church to continue its work during times of political unrest.

One way to remain welcome in the countries where the church serves is to send only well-qualified workers. More and more foreign governments insist that incoming missionaries have appropriate degrees (a bachelor's degree or higher).

Mission schools have done their work well in training nationals to lead and serve their own people. In countries that bar foreign missionaries, national workers carry on the work of the church.

Christian missions continue to promote the physical and spiritual well-being of millions. Alive and well, missions demonstrate love in action. Sanctified love for God's children everywhere is the basis for people helping people.

Spreading the Word: Evangelistic Media

3

"Go ye into all the world, and preach the gospel to every creature" (Mark 16:15).

What is the gospel? It is the good news of a loving, merciful, personal God and His Son, the risen Saviour. In proclaiming this gospel to all who will heed it, Adventists use today's modern print and electronic media.

Publishing Work

The Seventh-day Adventist publishing work began after Ellen White's vision at Dorchester, Massachusetts in November 1848. In describing it to her husband she said:

"You must begin to print a little paper and send it out to the people. Let it be small at first; but as the people read, they will send you means with which to print, and it will be a success from the first. From this small beginning it was shown to me to be like streams of light that went clear round the world" (*Life Sketches*, p. 125).

In July 1849, James White published, on credit, 1,000 copies of the first such little paper. Today Adventist presses produce periodicals, tracts, Bible study materials, Vacation Bible School lessons, children's books, textbooks, and devotional and doctrinal books. These meet personal as well as outreach needs.

Some of these publishing houses issue materials in more than one language. A few publish in as many as 10 or even 20 languages.

In general, the church-owned presses publish inspirational, educational, and doctrinal materials. Many of them put out an edition of the *Adventist Review* and the *Signs of the Times* or other evangelistic journal, and often a health magazine. Most of them produce the Bible lesson pamphlets (quarterlies) used each week in the Sabbath school.

Distribution Systems. The books and periodicals produced by the church's publishing houses are distributed through Adventist Book Centers and by literature evangelists.

Adventist Book Centers (ABCs) are the primary outlets. They sell books, Bibles and Bible study helps, missionary stories, records and tapes, and specialty merchandise such as vegetarian-type foods. Frequently located near conference offices, ABCs sell to both individuals and congregations. The ABCs also handle orders for periodical subscriptions.

Since the 1870s church representatives called literature evangelists have gone from house to house selling health and religious books. They work on a commission basis.

U.S. Publishing Houses

Adventists operate two publishing houses in the United States—the Review and Herald Publishing Association (Hagerstown, Maryland) and Pacific Press Publishing Association (Boise, Idaho). Together they publish a wide range of books and periodicals, from doctrinal studies to books for beginning readers.

The Review and Herald Publishing Association is the oldest institution of the Seventh-day Adventist Church. It is the outgrowth of the publishing work that began with that first paper James White had printed in Middletown, Connecticut, in 1849. In 1855 the institution established quarters in Battle Creek, Michigan. After fire totally destroyed its plant in 1902, the publishing house moved to Washington, D.C. (1903). More recently (1983) it relocated in Hagerstown, Maryland. Using modern technology it publishes periodicals, tracts, and evangelistic visual aids, as well as religious, health, and educational books.

The Pacific Press Publishing Association began operations in Oakland, California (1875), later moving to Mountain View, California (1904), and then to Nampa, Idaho (1984). Pacific Press publishes in 23 languages. From its modern high-speed presses come periodicals and books, including SDA elementary school textbooks, paperbacks, and books by Ellen G. White.

Periodicals. The two publishing houses produce materials used weekly in Sabbath schools. These include the weekly take-home papers (*Insight* for teens, *Guide* for juniors, *Primary Treasure* and *Our Little Friend* for younger children), as well as the Sabbath school quarterlies and helps for teachers and program leaders.

Other periodicals serve specialized audiences. For educators, *The Journal of Adventist Education;* for pastors, *Ministry;* for those interested in preserving religious liberty, *Liberty;* for temperance/antidrug education, *Listen* for teens and *The Winner* for younger children; for the health-minded, *Vibrant Life. The Seventh-day Adventist Periodical Index* indexes the church's major periodicals.

Missionary Journals. Missionary journals such as *Signs of the Times, Message,* and *Shabbat Shalom* aid the church in spiritual outreach, often through gift subscriptions. *Signs of the Times* appears in many languages around the world, although its content and format may vary.

Christian Record. The Christian Record Braille Foundation (Lincoln, Nebraska) is a specialized publishing house serving the sight- and hearing-impaired. Public contributions help support its activities. A yearly offering taken in North American Adventist churches also aids its work.

Christian Record publishes books, Bibles, and educational and religious materials in large print and in braille. It operates a lending library of more than 800 books recorded on cassette tapes. Other services include a Bible correspondence school, and camps for blind children. In North America a hundred district representatives make home visits to the blind.

Radio Ministries

Radio ministries range from the church-operated Voice of Prophecy to self-supporting broadcasts such as the Quiet Hour and local programs.

Since 1942 the Voice of Prophecy has broadcast coast to coast to American audiences on Sundays. It now broadcasts on weekdays, too. Broadcasts bearing the same name and focus are heard in many languages around the world. Staff members conduct evangelistic crusades and speak at Adventist camp meetings. The *Voice of Prophecy* and other SDA broadcasts offer Bible and health correspondence courses.

The *Quiet Hour* depends entirely on donations from listeners. This program's speakers conduct evangelistic crusades in the Far East. Its sister telecast is called *Search.*

Adventist World Radio (AWR) reaches many areas where local broadcasting is not possible. Begun in 1971 and operating for a limited time daily, its stations cover large areas of the world. Programming is in a variety of formats and languages.

The United States-based Adventist Radio Network is a loose-knit organization of SDA college radio stations. These beam inspirational and public-service programming to their communities.

Additionally, some pastors and congregations reach local audiences with brief spots, five-minute messages, and longer presentations. The Communication Department of the General Conference prepares scripts for such use.

Television Ministries

In the United States the church subsidizes the television programs produced by Faith for Today (established 1950), It Is Written (established 1956), and Breath of Life (established 1974). The telecasts differ in format and viewing audience.

Bible Correspondence Courses

The radio and television ministries offer free Bible and health correspondence courses, with some Bible courses in languages other than English. Bible guides for juniors and youth are also available.

Through these varied means—printed matter, radio programs, and telecasts—the Adventist Church spreads the good news about Jesus.

Helping Hand:

Serving the Community

4 "Time is short. Let the little time you have be employed for your own present and eternal good by active Christian service, doing all the good possible" (Ellen White, *The Upward Look,* p. 151).

In the spirit of neighborliness, Adventists offer a

variety of health, welfare, and community services. In practical ways they seek to follow the example of Christ.

Community Service Ministries

Collectively Adventists possess a multitude of God-given abilities and interests. They also have considerable skill in numerous professions, trades, hobbies, and crafts. These they use informally or professionally in serving others on a day-to-day basis.

Virtually every Seventh-day Adventist church conducts a Community Services outreach program that includes giving food, clothing, bedding, and household items to people who are suffering a temporary emergency. Whether housed in a single storage room or in a large building valued at many thousands of dollars, these church-operated Community Services centers offer many types of help to the community.

Here knowledgeable volunteers teach seminars in healthful diet, stress control, weight reduction, and overcoming habits involving tobacco and alcohol. Adventists have a keen interest in health. They desire to share what they know with others. Spiritual help and other classes are available too.

Disaster Relief. In times of disaster Community Services centers and their volunteers cooperate with disaster-related agencies such as Red Cross and Civil Defense in relieving disaster victims.

The overflow of supplies at Community Services centers is boxed and shipped to ADRA (Adventist Development and Relief Agency) warehouses at either United States coast. When large disasters occur and local church groups cannot meet the emergency needs, these goods are quickly transported to the areas needing them.

The shipments vary. One load of goods sent to a jungle area included 4,000 machetes. A more typical shipment consists of food, clothing, tents, blankets, and medicines. These are sent as soon as transportation can be arranged. In many cases Adventist volunteers assist at the distribution site.

Annually the value of disaster relief sent to dozens of countries amounts to millions of dollars' worth of cash, food, and supplies. Adventist churches take up a yearly offering for this purpose. Donations also come from other sources.

ADRA works with other international relief organizations in developing long-range assistance programs. A project in Haiti feeds 30,000. Other projects include building sanitary facilities and fishponds and conducting cooking schools and family planning sessions.

Improving the Standard of Living. In primitive areas of the world, ADRA focuses attention on primary health needs such as pure water and better sanitation. Along with the basic principles of sanitation and simple health self-care, the poor learn how to garden and prepare food, and also how to eat a proper diet. Improved farming methods and better seed work wonders too. In one place people "farmed" with pointed sticks. By switching to the ordinary garden hoe, they doubled their crop production. For them that made the difference between famine and surplus.

ADRA also provides education in needed work skills, efficient work habits, basic literacy, and money management.

Health Work

Many Adventists have chosen to become health-care professionals. The church, through its medical university and numerous schools of nursing, has trained a significant number of those who now serve in its medical work.

The denomination's health-care system began in 1866 with the opening of the Western Health Reform Institute, a forerunner of Battle Creek Sanitarium in Battle Creek, Michigan. Today Adventist clinics and hospitals scattered around the world administer high-quality care. In less-developed nations this kind of care brings high-ranking government officials to Adventist hospitals as patients.

While some Adventist medical institutions provide

mostly general care, some are very specialized. Campo Grande Adventist Hospital in Brazil treats patients who have an endemic skin disease called savage fire or wildfire *(pemphigus foliaceus).* Fatal if not treated, this disease causes skin and mouth blisters. Victims die from infection or starvation.

This hospital traces its beginnings to 1948 when an Adventist began treating wildfire victims with the medication that had cured his wife of this disease. By 1952 a hospital had been built to house those who came for treatment. The current treatment, used with corticosteroids, antibiotics, and a better diet, has greatly increased the number of complete regressions and reduced the death rate.

In the United States small lifestyle reconditioning centers offer personalized instruction and therapy. Live-in programs lasting three weeks help participants to lose weight, depend less on prescription drugs, and make health-promoting lifestyle changes. Improved diet and regular exercise are stressed. These health centers are not funded by the church.

Common to Adventist health ministries in all their forms is emphasis on the eight natural remedies outlined many years ago by Ellen White—pure air, sunlight, abstemiousness (temperance), rest, exercise, proper diet, the use of water, and trust in divine power.

Mission Hospitals. Mission hospitals such as Monument Valley Adventist Hospital in Utah are another example of how the Adventist Church serves the community. This service to the Navajo Indians began with a clinic in a trailer (1950). A hospital followed (1961). In a recent year it provided acute care to some 500 patients, and outpatient care to more than 10,000 persons. The nearest clinics are 25 miles distant, with the closest hospital 100 miles away.

The hospital also operates an ambulance (staffed by volunteers from the hospital) and a small used-clothing outlet. Since few homes in the area have electricity and running water, the hospital provides a launderette, shower facilities, and water from its well.

Temperance. In the Adventist view, temperance is more than refraining from the use of alcoholic beverages. It includes abstaining from tobacco, tea, coffee, and all injurious or addictive drugs and chemicals. It means self-control and moderation. Persons who live temperately can avoid much disease and misery.

The Adventist-sponsored International Commission for the Prevention of Alcoholism and Drug Dependency (ICPA) works with government officials in various countries, promoting temperate living and freedom from drug abuse. International congresses, lectures, and temperance materials further this work.

Adventists are glad to give their neighbors a helping hand. Adventists respond to the needs around them. That's what Jesus would do.

Training for Service:

Christian Education

5 True education "is the harmonious development of the physical, the mental, and the spiritual powers. It prepares the student for the joy of service in this world and for the higher joy of wider service in the world to come" (Ellen White, *Education,* p. 13).

Adventists believe in Christian education. Their denomination's school system is said to be the largest network of Protestant schools in the world. As a rule, the denominationally-sponsored high schools and colleges in the United States are fully accredited. Their facilities, curriculum, and staff meet government standards. Academically most students perform at or above the norm.

Purpose of Christian Education

Christian education aims to help students know, love, and accept Christ as their personal Saviour. In addition, Adventist schools teach a biblical view of human origin, mission, and destiny.

Christian education strives to be Christ-centered. Adventists believe a balanced education that develops the mental, physical, spiritual, and social capacities is needed to prepare students for life both here and hereafter. Adventist schools seek to instill sound moral principles and Christian character in each student and to reinforce the family's spiritual values.

Using a Christ-centered curriculum, Christian teachers teach by precept and example. A nurturing spiritual atmosphere helps students mature and develop a strong commitment to serving God. Parochial schools help students formulate their Christian ideals, philosophy of life, and concept of service.

The Christian Home

Parents know and love their child as few others do. They have the privilege of setting the stage for the child's success (or failure) later in life. As the first teachers, parents guide the child's character development and build his/her feelings of self-worth.

Ellen White advised parents to let children run free as lambs (not physically confined or restrained by formal education) until the age of 8 or 10. Educators find that many 6- and 7-year-olds lack the eye-hand coordination usually required of them in the classroom. Young children also have very short attention spans.

Knowing this, some parents delay the child's entrance into first grade. They allow the child to explore, ask questions, and solve practical problems. Parents can provide a home environment rich in learning experiences, books, and the natural sciences. Much can be taught—and learned—informally.

The School and Curriculum

In Adventist grade schools a typical day begins with a devotional time, Bible reading, singing, and prayer. A Bible lesson follows. Students spend most of the day studying math, social studies, science, language arts, music, and other customary academic subjects.

Adventist schools teach the biblical Creation as counter to the theory of evolution, which denies the creatorship of God. Students discover that God created them on purpose and for a purpose. This adds to their sense of self-worth.

School libraries emphasize biographies, true-to-life stories, natural science, missions, and other factual resource books. Denominational reading texts inform while developing reading skills and literature appreciation. Textbooks published by secular companies usually receive careful examination before they are approved for use.

Academy (high school) and college students participate in regular worship and religious assemblies (chapel). Bible courses are requisite for graduation. Interested students have opportunities to share their beliefs with others through campus organizations and activities.

The Financial Picture

Adventists finance their schools by tuition fees, supplemented with subsidies from the local congregation and conference. Scholarships and grants to worthy students assist some families and students.

A part-time job in a school-operated industry enables many college and academy students to earn a portion of their school expenses. Varying from campus to campus, these industries range from glassworks, bakeries, and dairy farms to greenhouses, strawberry fields, and furniture factories. Students also do meaningful paid work in the school cafeteria, dormitories, offices, janitorial, and other departments.

The Work-Study Advantage

Earning all or part of their school expenses lets students experience the dignity of labor. They can also develop good work habits and learn important job skills. As a bonus, they discover what employers expect from employees. A moderate amount of labor also seems to boost academic achievement. The work-study program has other benefits. It combines theory and practice, builds self-confidence, and makes education more relevant to life in the real world.

Extracurricular Activities

Adventist schools de-emphasize contact sports and exciting amusements. Sports contests between schools are the exception rather than the norm. Although excessive competition is discouraged, exercise and physical fitness are promoted.

In addition to study, work, and worship, Adventist schools provide many opportunities for social interaction and group involvement. Music ensembles and gymnastics are popular activities.

A Word About Public Schools

Adventists appreciate the public schools and the excellent work they do. Many communities operate top-notch schools with well-trained, highly competent staffs. Public schools offer excellent job training. They turn out skilled craftsmen and competent professionals.

Couldn't these tax-supported public schools adequately train the church's young people? Intellectually, yes. Yet secular education's emphasis on human philosophies and goals tends to weaken rather than strengthen Christian commitment and standards. So for philosophical, spiritual, and moral reasons Adventists find it best to train their young people in their own schools. The Adventist goal of a thorough moral and religious education for their children is beyond the scope of tax-supported public education.

The moral standards and lifestyles of peers and available adult role models also influence the student. These can either reinforce or undermine the student's home training and the family's Christian values. Role models make a decided difference.

Whereas Adventist schools reserve the Sabbath hours for worship and other religious activities, secular schools routinely schedule sports and major social events for Friday night and Saturday. This bars conscientious young Sabbathkeepers from participating in a number of worthwhile school activities.

Secular literature and reading textbooks draw heavily from fictional works that are not true to life or in keeping with biblical values. These books create a taste for the titillating, the exciting, the fanciful. Many authors' lives reflect values that are decidedly unchristian. Since young students are so impressionable, Adventists prefer to introduce literature that, while protecting young minds from the seamy side of the world for which they are not ready, develops evaluative skills and creates a taste for that which is true, pure, and lovely.

What happens when the home and the school do not teach the same standards and principles? Ruth Murdoch is paraphrased as saying, "Children need to find consistency of opinions between home and school. This is especially true of religion, recreation, dress, and ethics; otherwise they get confused" (Pietro Copiz, "Dimensions of Adventist Education," *Adventist Review,* Apr. 14, 1983).

All in all, Adventists feel there is, Pietro Copiz says, a "substantial spiritual gamble in attending public schools" *(ibid.).* Rather than gamble with their offspring's eternal future, many Adventist parents choose to provide a high-quality Christian education for their youth.

Then Why Christian Education?

Adventist parents anticipate an eternal life with Christ, and they earnestly desire to have their entire family there. That's one reason so many parents and churches sacrifice in order to provide Christian schools for their youth. They realize that what students don't learn can be just as important as what they do learn.

"Train up a child in the way he should go," reads the ancient proverb, "and when he is old, he will not depart from it" (Prov. 22:6). A system of thorough Christian education helps the Christian home in this training.

PART THREE

A Global Church

Christ commanded His followers to "make disciples of all nations, baptizing them . . . , teaching them" (Matt. 28:19, 20, RSV).

The Seventh-day Adventist Church has taken this injunction seriously. Its work reaches around the globe.

What's a GC?

Church Organization

6 "The church [God's called-out ones] is God's appointed agency for the salvation of men. It was organized for service, and its mission is to carry the gospel to the world" (Ellen White, *The Acts of the Apostles,* p. 9).

The Adventist movement of the 1840s had neither name nor organizational structure. As the body of Sabbathkeepers grew and flourished, however, problems arose. One, the lack of legal identity and a name, meant the religious movement could not hold title to property.

Another problem, that of self-appointed preachers who preached with more zeal than integrity and consecration, called for an effective way of controlling who would preach from the pulpits. Officially organizing as a denomination helped solve these and other problems.

First came the name, Seventh-day Adventist. Then, incorporation of the publishing association, followed by a form of church organization and a plan for licensing and identifying authorized ministers. The first General Conference met in Battle Creek, Michigan, in 1863 and framed a constitution. Denominational headquarters were established there. Both the publishing plant and the church headquarters moved to Washington, D.C., in 1903.

Today the Seventh-day Adventist Church is an international organization. Its structure enables it to operate and support an extensive and varied work around the world.

The church operates on the principle of persuasion. A board of trustees or an executive committee governs every branch of church endeavor and every level of its structure. The group, rather than an individual, has the final say in matters of importance.

Adventist Church structure has four levels: the General Conference and its divisions, union conferences, local conferences, and local churches (see figures 1 and 2). At each of these levels a legally incorporated body acts as trustee for church-owned properties. These corporations receive gifts and legacies and hold title to property.

The General Conference

The constitution of the General Conference of Seventh-day Adventists declares that the church's object "is to teach all nations the everlasting gospel of our Lord and Saviour Jesus Christ and the commandments of God." Territorially, the General Conference takes in all the land areas of the world.

While in its strictest sense the name General Conference (GC for short) refers to the Adventist world headquarters and its staff, it is also used as shorthand for the church in plenary session—the General Conference conference, if you will.

World General Conference Sessions

Every five years delegates from around the world (some 1,800 at a recent GC) assemble for a General Conference session. They report needs as well as progress. The proceedings are translated into the major languages of the delegates. Delegates elect about 300 church leaders, take care of business, set policies, and settle doctrinal issues. The General Conference president, assisted by the GC vice presidents, presides at the GC sessions.

Changes in the *Church Manual* are voted only at General Conference sessions but they first receive careful study in committee. Adhering to one church manual and operating under one general policy help to unify the church.

The *Adventist Review* publishes a daily report of the General Conference proceedings. These capture the international flavor and excitement of the session. Many features help draw large crowds to the general meetings. These include mission pageants, and displays and exhibits by the church's North American universities, publishing houses, and overseas divisions. Special musical programs add to the enjoyment.

The General Conference: Administrative Center

GC officers oversee the church's world work from offices in Washington, D.C., and Takoma Park, Maryland. Vice presidents serve either as general administrative assistants to the president or as presidents of world divisions. Among other duties, GC officers chair committees, give counsel, and promote church unity.

The General Conference selects, sends, and supports foreign missionaries. Its income comes from tithe, offerings given for missions, and other sources.

General Conference Executive Committee

Between GC sessions the Executive Committee administers the church. It meets weekly. Chaired by the GC president or one of the general vice-presidents, it has the authority to transact denominational business. It can grant or withdraw the credentials or licenses of its workers and fill vacancies that occur on the GC level.

International in membership, the GC Executive Committee has a broad view of church affairs. Its members represent union conferences, union missions, schools, departments, institutions, and other subsidiary organizations. The committee deals with recommendations coming from other, smaller committees.

Annual Council

The Executive Committee meets in council annually in October. This council adopts the yearly budget, appropriating funds for new and established mission projects. It sets the offering calendar and designates which divisions will receive special project funds from the Thirteenth Sabbath Offering. Problems and questions from unions and local conferences appear on the council's agenda. The Annual Council can make changes in the working policy of the General Conference.

General Conference Departments

The departments represent branches of church ministry. Elected directors, chosen for their experience, capabilities, and interests, serve as resource people and specialized leaders. The departments include Church Ministries, Communication, Education, Health and Temperance, Public Affairs and Religious Liberty, and Publishing. They foster important aspects of denominational work. Departments are advisory rather than administrative.

Along with counsel and workshops, certain GC departments generate resource materials and departmental publications. For example, the Church Ministries Department publishes songbooks, Sabbath school lesson quarterlies, Vacation Bible School materials, and child evangelism aids.

Divisions of the General Conference

For administrative purposes the General Conference is organized into major divisions. They are: Africa-Indian Ocean, Eastern Africa, Euro-Africa, Far Eastern, Inter-American, North American, South American, South Pacific, Southern Asia, and Trans-European. Divisions are made up of union conferences and their respective missions and/or local conferences.

Each division has its own officers and executive committee. In theory, each division is a GC section operating in a particular geographical area. Divisions are not a separate level of organization but in a sense, GC branch offices made necessary by national languages and geography.

Divisions handle their own finances, personnel, institutions, and licensing.

Union Conferences

Next come the union conferences. In the North American Division, each of the nine union conferences covers four or more states or provinces. An executive committee regulates union conference affairs.

Union conferences hold legal title to and operate the church-owned institutions (colleges, for example) that serve their territory. Each union also publishes a newsmagazine for its constituents.

Departmental leaders serve as resource persons for their conferences, local congregations, and other church entities. They cooperate with their counterparts in the division.

Local Conferences

In the United States a local conference may consist of one or more states or parts of states. Geographical features and membership demographics help set the conference's boundaries. In those parts of the world where local funds are inadequate for self-support, instead of conferences there are missions, or sections, as they may be called.

The conference's executive committee operates between the triennial constituency meetings. It employs and transfers ministerial employees and manages the budget.

Conferences employ evangelists, pastors, teachers, Bible workers, and administrators. They also issue and renew licenses, credentials, and certificates. Further, they assign and support pastors, subsidize parochial schools, and operate parochial high schools and youth camps. They also actively promote evangelism and personal witnessing. Conferences sponsor the yearly camp meetings. The conference corporation holds legal title to properties such as schools and churches.

Conference Departments

Like the GC departments, those at the local conference level are channels for ideas, resources, training, and support. They serve congregations, pastors, and individuals.

The Communication Department encourages the local church in increasing public awareness of the denomination's work and purpose. News releases and county fair exhibits are examples of this. The conference Trust Department handles charitable giving through estates and wills.

The Youth Department operates the conference youth camp. It also trains leaders for local Pathfinder youth clubs and holds conference-wide youth events. The Publishing Department trains and encourages literature evangelists in their door-to-door ministry of the printed page.

The Education Department head superintends the conference's elementary and secondary schools. The Health and Temperance Department promotes public seminars on health, such as on diet and drug-free living. Antidrug programs include the 4 DK Plan: Four-Dimensional Key to the Cause of Alcoholism, and the Breathe-Free Plan to Stop Smoking. This department makes relevant seminar materials (such as films, posters, and other audiovisual aids) available.

Figure 1.

General Structure of the
Seventh-day Adventist Church

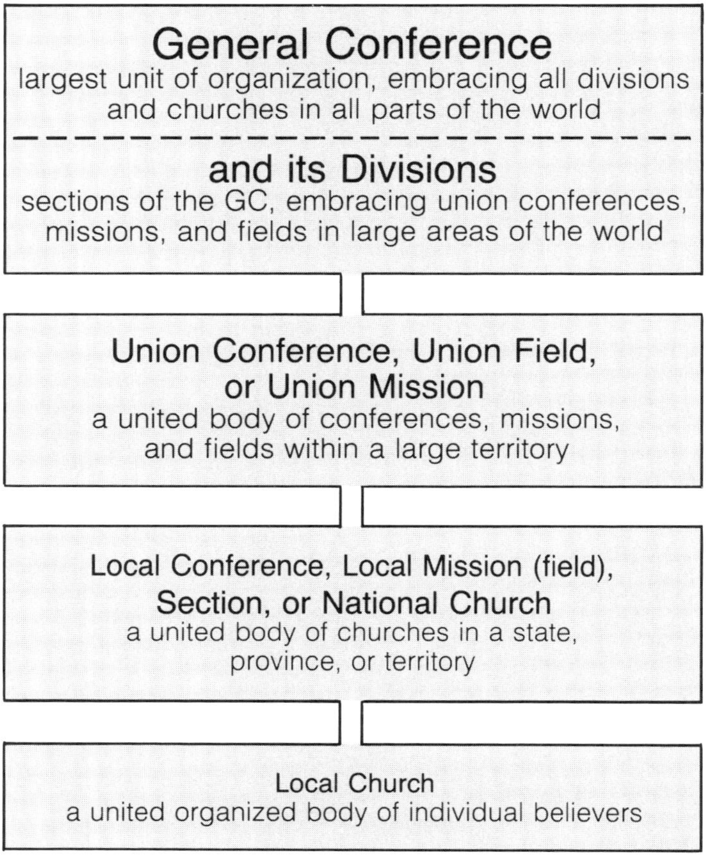

Note: A mission field is similar to a conference but its major officers are elected by the next higher body. The same is true of the union mission. The several attached fields do not fit into this organizational pattern; they are instead under the "wing" of a division or even the GC. Missions that meet certain requirements of leadership, cooperation, a well-balanced program of church activities, financial stability, etc. may be granted conference or union conference status.

(Sources: *Church Manual,* 1981 ed., p. 54; *SDA Encyclopedia,* rev. ed.)

Figure 2.

Example of SDA Church Structure

	Example:
General Conference (the land area of the world) — and its Divisions (all or part of a continent)	North American Division (Canada and the United States)
Union Conference (a cluster of states, provinces, or countries)	North Pacific Union Conference (Alaska, Idaho, Montana, Oregon, and Washington)
Local Conference (usually all or part of a state)	Washington Conference (most of Washington State west of the Cascade Mountains)
Local Church (area may include all or part of a city and/or county)	(Washington Conference has 71 congregations, with a total of more than 12,000 members)

Note: The North American Division is operated from the General Conference headquarters. This is the exception rather than the rule.

Each local conference is subdivided into districts of one or more congregations. Pastoral assignments vary. Some pastors lead several small churches. In a large district or congregation, two or more pastors may provide the leadership.

Congregations

At the grassroots of the Adventist Church, thousands of believers actively support it and participate in community outreach.

The congregation nominates and elects new officers yearly. The *Church Manual* outlines their duties, as well as the structure and scope of the suborganizations. Local elders lead out in public worship and assist the pastor. Deacons serve the congregation, caring for church property; with deaconesses, deacons have a special duty to the poor, the unfortunate, and the needy sick. Deacons and deaconesses assist during baptismal and Communion services.

The Sabbath school superintendent manages the entire Sabbath school and may also lead out in the weekly adult program. The personal ministries leader encourages various forms of witnessing and spiritual outreach. The Community Services leader directs health and welfare programs aimed at meeting local needs.

The church board, composed of key elected officers, transacts the congregation's business. This body or a separate school board operates the local parochial school.

So what's a GC? It's the underlying international organization with a worldwide view of the work to be done. It's the smooth-running machine that helps the Seventh-day Adventist Church make disciples in all nations.

Where the Money Comes From:

Christian Stewardship

7 "Bring the whole tithe into the storehouse, that there may be food in my house. Test me in this and see if I will not throw open the floodgates of heaven and pour out so much blessing that you will not have room enough for it. I will prevent pests from devouring your crops, and the vines in your fields will not cast their fruit" (Mal. 3:10, 11, NIV).

According to one story, two traveling Adventists chanced to meet in the middle of a desert. They quickly formed a committee and took up an offering!

Adventists do believe in organization. And they do give often and generously to Christian work. But how can they do it? Through consistent Christian stewardship. Again and again they have tested the promise of Malachi 3.

Stewardship

Stewardship is the management of another's goods. It is a relationship between owner and caretaker. The caretaker may have use of the property, and the owner may allow him a certain percentage of the profits.

God is the Creator-Owner of all things. We are caretakers, or managers, of property that is not ours. He gives us a 90 percent commission, claiming only 10 percent for Himself. He has a right to receive His percentage first.

Tithing demonstrates a person's loyalty and commitment to God. The faithful caretaker does not covet or mismanage another's property.

In this steward relationship, God creates a climate for trust and obedience. Can each trust the other to be faithful and honest? The steward relationship reveals whom God can trust with greater responsibilities and eternal riches.

God wants wholehearted, willing, cheerful service. Such servants find peace instead of worry, faith instead of fear, joy instead of guilt. From their own portion (the 90 percent) they express their love and gratitude through freewill gifts that aid in God's work on earth.

In giving humans dominion over the earth (Gen. 1:26) God did not relinquish ownership. Rather, He made humans responsible for wisely managing His property. As owner, He restricted its use, requiring His managers (stewards or guardians) to return to Him one tenth of the increase (income). Thus they would acknowledge God as the true owner.

God's people have a duty to use their time, talents, and treasures wisely and unselfishly and to follow His instructions exactly. They dare not disregard their known duty. Through either faithful or unfaithful management they reveal their spiritual health and relationship with God.

Tithes and Offerings

The biblical practice of tithing acknowledges God's ownership. God claims a tithe (one tenth) of each person's income. Already belonging to God, tithe is returned to Him rather than paid to Him. The tithe principle is a tenet of the Seventh-day Adventist Church.

How should the tithe be figured? Wage earners calculate the tithe on their income. They are encouraged to tithe the full salary or earnings before income taxes and other deductions. The tithe on a gross income of $100 would be $10. Self-employed persons and owners of businesses figure tithe on their profit, the amount left after deducting their business expenses. The tithe principle applies to garden produce, livestock, and other kinds of increase, as well as wages. (Ask your conference for the booklet *Tithing Principles and Guidelines.)*

It is advisable to write the tithe check first, immediately after banking the paycheck or other income. This safeguards against forgetting to return the tithe or misusing it, such as diverting it to living expenses.

The local conference provides printed tithe and offering envelopes. Members mark these to show the amount and intended purpose of the money enclosed (see Figure 3: Marked Tithe and Offering Envelope). Receipts are issued periodically. Tithe is ordinarily channeled through the local church that holds the person's membership.

The 90 Percent. Can 90 percent provide life's necessities? Yes, as generations of faithful tithers have discovered. Tithing helps people learn to handle money wisely. It aids in stemming selfishness, and also encourages an attitude of gratitude toward God. As promised, He opens the floodgates of heaven and pours out blessings.

Careful selection of affordable merchandise helps many people manage on the 90 percent. Good stewards find it best to choose good-quality items and only what is actually needed. Sometimes members choose to delay purchases or do without so they can support the church financially.

Offerings. Freewill offerings supply funds needed by a wide range of health-care, educational, and other types of religious work around the world. The tithe is 10 percent of income, but the size of freewill offerings is an individual matter. Some congregations suggest specific percentages for the church budget and the World Budget offerings. Compliance is voluntary. Anciently, God's people gave 25 percent (10 percent tithe and 15 percent for offerings) of their increase and were greatly blessed for it. Today some voluntarily give 20 to 30 percent of their income for God's work.

Many congregations follow the Personal Giving Plan. Authorized and approved by the North American Division of the church, it provides systematic support for the local church, the local conference, and the world church (see Figure 4: Personal Giving Plan Envelope). This plan covers all offerings except Ingathering and Investment. In addition to the tithe (10 percent) the giving guide suggests the following percentages: world mission budget, 2 to 3 percent; conference budget, 1 to 2 percent: and local church budget, 7 to 10 percent.

Adventists pay taxes to support public schools. Though often not wealthy, many Adventists find that God's blessing on the 90 percent remaining of their income after tithe enables them to provide for their own needs and to fund numerous Christian causes in addition to Christian education.

The local churches receive tithes and offerings each week. They retain funds earmarked for local needs and remit the rest to the local conference.

General Conference Budget

The General Conference world budget funds come mostly from mission offerings and tithe. Sabbath school offerings provide about 21 percent, and world tithe about 59 percent. In general, funds shared with the General Conference by the North American Division supplement the budgets of overseas fields. A portion of the yearly public solicitation known as Ingathering augments the General Conference budget. Tithe supports ministers and certain other denominational employees around the world. Freewill offerings supply capital to build and operate churches, schools, hospitals, and other work.

The GC budget provides operating and special capital appropriations to the church's world divisions and General Conference institutions such as Andrews University, Loma Linda University, Oakwood College, and the Adventist Media Center. Thus the GC supplements the budgets of organizations that cannot yet fully support themselves.

Each local conference regularly sends 10 percent or

Figure 3.

Marked Tithe and Offering Envelope

TITHES AND OFFERINGS

Name ____________________

Address ____________________

City ____________________ Zip __________

Date __________ Rec. No. __________

CONFERENCE FUNDS

TITHE (10% of Income)	$ 10 –
Ingathering — Donated	$
Ingathering — Solicited	$
World Mission Offerings	$
Sabbath School	$ 3 –
Evangelism	$ 1 –
UNITED DEVELOPMENT FUND	$
	$
	$
	$
	$

LOCAL CHURCH FUNDS

CHURCH BUDGET	$ 7 –
Church Expense	$
Church School	$
Sabbath School Expense	$
Lay Activities	$
BUILDING FUND	$
NEW SCHOOL BUILDING FUND	$
	$
TOTAL ENCLOSED	$ 21 –

Washington Conference of Seventh-day Adventists
P.O. Box 1008 — Bothell, Washington 98011

Based on $100 income. The offerings marked on the Figure 3 envelope will vary according to offerings scheduled and the individual's preferences.

Figure 4.

Personal Giving Plan Envelope

Name ______________________________

Address ______________________________

City ____________________ Date ______________

TITHE

and Offerings of Love to God

Tithe	$ 10 —
World Missions	$ 3 —
	$
	$
	$
Rocky Mountain Advance	$ 1 —
	$
Church Budget	$ 7 —
DEVELOPMENT FUND	$
	$
	$
Total Enclosed	$ 21 —

Rocky Mountain Conference
of Seventh-day Adventists
2520 South Downing
Denver, Colorado 80210

Figure 5.

How Tithe Is Shared

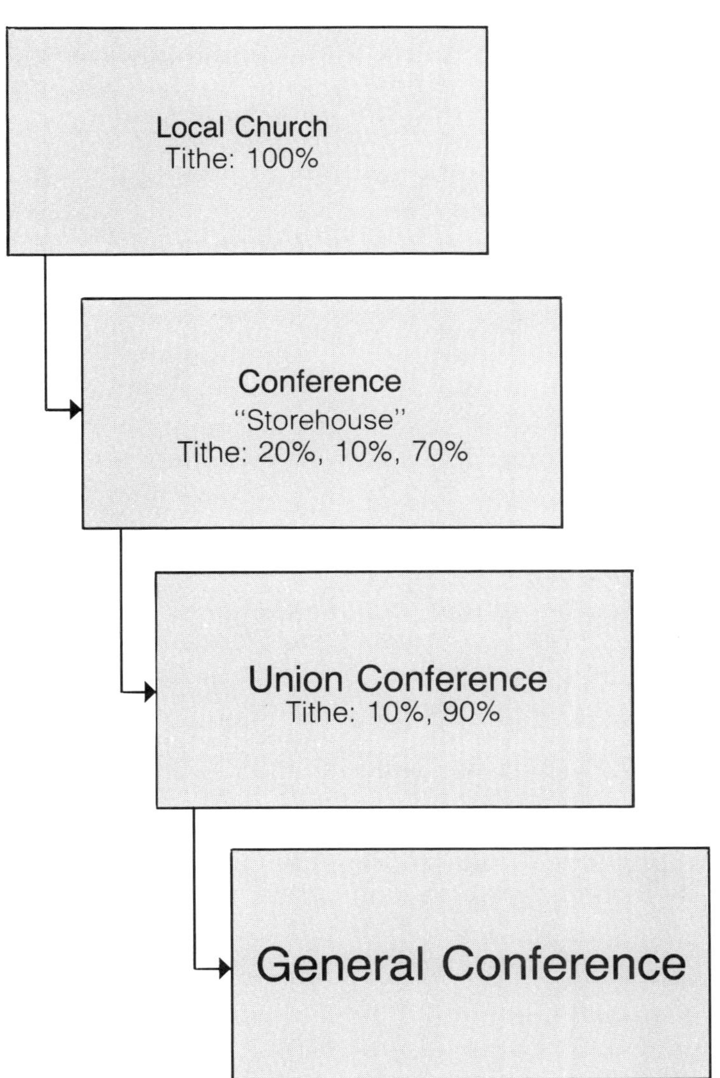

more of its tithe to the union conference. Then the local conference pays its pastors, administrators, and certain other employees from remaining tithe funds. Union conferences and divisions handle tithe funds similarly. Ultimately a portion of the tithe reaches the General Conference treasury (see Figure 5: How Tithe Is Shared).

In North America a remuneration schedule that applies to all denominational employees allows for modest recognition of responsibilities borne, educational qualifications, previous experience, and years of service. Provision has also been made to assist employees on health-care and children's educational expenses. A congregation's location, size, and finances do not affect its pastor's salary.

The GC General Retirement Plan supports the denomination's eligible retired employees and their surviving spouses and dependent children. Conferences, colleges, hospitals, and other employing organizations within the church contribute to this plan.

Major Offerings. The Annual Council sets the schedule for major church offerings that flow into the GC budget or go to General Conference institutions or specific ministries (see Figure 6: Offering Schedule in Local Churches). This schedule includes:

* Adventist World Radio—Overseas shortwave radio ministry.
* Christian Record Braille Foundation—Christian sound, braille, and large-print materials for the blind and visually impaired.
* Disaster and Famine Relief—Emergency assistance for large-scale disasters around the world.
* Adventist Television Ministries—The television programs produced by Breath of Life, Faith For Today, and It Is Written. Targeted to reach specific cultural and ethnic groups.
* Health and Temperance Offering—shared by the local conference, union, and GC. Used for Breathe-Free plans, antidrug education, and similar programs.

* Inner City—Ministry to needy people in the cities.
* North American Missions—Special help for Native American work.
* Missions Extension, Annual Sacrifice—Major mission offerings that go into the GC budget.
* Religious Liberty—Religious liberty issues and the rights of religious minorities brought into public notice through subscriptions to *Liberty* magazine. Champions the separation of church and state and the right of individuals to follow their own conscience. At the conference level, funds legal defense in religious discrimination cases.
* Servicemen's Literature—Offering for church papers and religious reading materials sent to Seventh-day Adventists in military service.
* Voice of Prophecy—Radio outreach ministry.

Oakwood College receives an annual offering. Loma Linda University and Andrews University receive offerings in alternate years.

Conference development programs in the local conferences provide, from nontithe funds, money for specific needs that are of a conference-wide nature. For example: secondary and elementary school construction, secondary school operation, church building construction, youth camp facilities, camp meeting facilities, evangelistic equipment.

As individuals and as a church, Seventh-day Adventists have tested God's promise to pour out His blessings. They have truly found Him faithful to His promise.

Special Delivery:

A Messenger for the Last Days

8 "Believe in the Lord your God, so shall ye be established; believe his prophets, so shall ye prosper" (2 Chron. 20:20).

Adventists accept the biblical doctrine of spiritual gifts, including the gift of prophecy (see Rom. 12:6). They believe God has given their church a special messenger in the person of Ellen G. White (1827-1915). This godly woman's ministry has greatly influenced the SDA Church and its members.

Many times God gave her visions or dreams bearing timely counsel, reproof, warning, and/or encouragement for individuals or the church. In appropriate ways and at appropriate times she delivered these messages. Never claiming the title of prophetess, she instead called herself a messenger of God; in reality, her work was broader than that of a prophet.

She set an example of practical godliness and total commitment to her Lord and His work. Repeatedly she urged believers to study the Bible and discover God's truths for themselves.

At times her counsel seemed contrary to human wisdom. For instance, she urged that a medical school be established in California. Despite great obstacles the money was raised and the school established. An ambitious financial undertaking, Loma Linda University has been a great benefit in the church's medical work.

The basic principles outlined in her writings still apply, although the specifics may be outdated. For example, she advised girls to learn how to harness horses. Today's counterparts can profitably learn to drive a car and change a flat tire. Young men can benefit too from learning basic homemaking skills.

Christians young and old find her inspired insights helpful in character development and in victorious Christian living. Her books, written on many subjects and published in many languages, sell well even many decades after her death.

The woman herself is variously called E. G. White, Sister White, and Mrs. White. Her writings are often referred to as "the Spirit of Prophecy" and "the pen of inspiration."

The Place of Prophetic Guidance in the Church

Ellen White's counsels and inspirational writings have nurtured and united the Adventist Church. The church does not, however, elevate them above the Bible or equate them with it. Valuable as they are, they can never replace God's holy Scriptures. Recognizing this, she repeatedly urged the church to study God's Word, calling her writings a lesser light pointing to the Greater Light.

A Dedicated Life

Ellen Gould White (nee Harmon) and her fraternal twin, Elizabeth, were born near Gorham, Maine, on November 26, 1827, the youngest of eight children. Later the family moved to Portland, Maine, where her father made hats for a living.

When Ellen was 9, a stone thrown by a classmate struck her in the face, breaking her nose and apparently causing a concussion. For three weeks she lay in a state of unconsciousness. She recovered, but poor health prevented her from completing her formal education.

For some time she could not write because of her unsteady hand. Nor could she read, for reading made her dizzy. Yet by the time she died at age 87 she had written more than 100,000 pages and had 24 books in print, with two more ready to be published.

At the age of 14 she was baptized and became very interested in helping others know God better. Not long after her seventeenth birthday she received her first vision. God laid upon her the burden of sharing what He had revealed to her. This she did and brought encouragement to many.

In 1846 she married James White, an Adventist preacher. She bore him four sons. One son died in infancy, another in his teens. The other two became Adventist ministers. As Ellen and her husband traveled about building up the church, they made many personal sacrifices and endured numerous hardships.

One of the pioneer leaders of the Adventist Church, James edited and published papers and pamphlets. He died in 1881 at the age of 60. He had served as General Conference president for 10 years.

Now alone, Ellen continued with the work God had given her to do. For a time she lived in Europe and then Australia. Her labors helped establish the church in those places. In 1900 she settled near St. Helena, California, where she died in 1915. Writing (often at night), book preparation, and personal work filled her last years.

Her neighbors at St. Helena knew her as the woman who spoke so lovingly of Jesus. Her associates found her true to principle, a cheerful, dedicated servant of God, a wise counselor. Her family knew her as a devoted mother.

The Author and Speaker

Ellen White wrote on many vital topics. These included the redemptive work of Christ, child training, the home, Christian service, education, health, medical missionary work, temperance, and stewardship. She exhorted believers to persevere in their faith, clinging to Jesus.

She also wrote a commentary on human history,

sharing insights gained through revelation and personal study. These books, the five-volume Conflict of the Ages set, trace the course of history from Satan's fall to the ultimate triumph of good over evil.

Her work included the difficult task of delivering messages of rebuke and warning. Some recipients heeded her messages and repented; others did not. Nevertheless, she kept urging believers to commit their lives to God and trust wholly in Him, to obey His commands and thus become doers of the Word, as well as hearers.

A popular public speaker, she spoke at conferences, camp meetings, and churches. Upon learning she would speak, church members flocked in to hear her. Often she addressed large audiences, her clear voice carrying well, although there were no public address systems to help her. She enjoyed giving public lectures on Christian temperance.

A Health Emphasis

In June of 1863 a comprehensive health vision at Otsego, Michigan, gave her a broad view of health and preventive medicine. It touched on the causes of disease, rational treatment of the sick, child care, nutrition, and such topics as the harmful effects of stimulants and narcotics. Ellen White adopted a more healthful diet and better health practices and encouraged others to do so, too.

Doctors of that time treated disease with opium and poisonous drugs such as calomel and antimony. Many patients died from the treatment rather than the disease. Denouncing the use of these harmful drugs, Ellen White urged the use of rational remedies instead.

Scientific Verification

In recent years scientists have verified many of Ellen White's health views. In studying SDA dietary patterns and death rates, they discovered that Adventists have a significantly lower incidence of heart disease and death from cancer. One study showed that American Adventist men have a life expectancy six years longer than the average.

What has made the difference? Apparently lifestyle factors such as diet, a right relationship with God, and less stress. The human machine lasts longer when properly cared for.

Ellen White often counseled on matters of diet and health, warning against the use of specific items. Medical experts are still exploring the impact of the following:

Alcohol causes cirrhosis of the liver and destroys irreplaceable brain cells. It is a depressant and can cause birth defects if taken internally during pregnancy. Caffeine, an addictive substance in coffee, cola drinks, and some medications, raises the blood pressure and affects the nerves. Tobacco, harmful whether smoked or chewed, leads to lung and throat cancer. It also increases blood pressure.

Meat has been linked to cancer and other diseases. Meat lacks fiber; it stays in the intestinal tract longer, giving any cancer-causing substances (carcinogens) present more time to cause damage.

Too much protein and phosphorus in the diet leaches calcium from the bones, causing osteoporosis (brittle bones), so common in older women. The kidneys must work harder to throw off the additional waste products contained in meat. The cholesterol in foods of animal origin is suspected of contributing to heart disease.

Grease and fats are high in calories and difficult to digest. Certain toxic substances are known to lodge in the fatty tissues of animals. The eater's system must handle these. The overuse of sugar, high in calories, can lead to obesity as well as tooth decay. Sugar hampers the white blood cells' ability to fight infection. Salt, if used in excess, apparently plays a role in the development of high blood pressure.

The Good News in Health

Temperate, healthful eating and living can do much to reduce health risks and costs. For better health and clearer thinking, Ellen White recommended a vegetarian diet composed of a variety of high-quality fruits, vegetables, nuts, and whole grains prepared in a wholesome and simple manner. Such a diet offers many pluses.

At a time when dietary supplements were unknown, Ellen White told how to obtain needed nutrients and maintain health. Eat greens, she said. Be much in the open air and sunshine. Exercise.

We know now that leafy green vegetables contain calcium, vitamin A, and fiber. The body uses sunlight to manufacture vitamin D. An adequate supply of calcium in the diet, when combined with exercise and vitamin D, keeps bones strong and delays the onset of osteoporosis. Other combinations of nutrients likely prevent other heath problems, too.

Other recommendations included country living, exercise for sedentary workers, an abundance of fresh air and pure water, regularity in eating and sleeping, and observing the weekly Sabbath. These factors tend to reduce physical and mental stress.

Other Counsel

As one who encouraged others to be faithful stewards in all things, Ellen White set an admirable example. In addition to returning her tithe, she supported the church generously with offerings. Sometimes when she did not have the cash, she borrowed money to help an institution meet its mortgage payments. She did this gladly, to advance the cause she so dearly loved. She gave the profits from several of her books to help get many sanitariums and schools out of debt.

Living economically allowed her to take in sick people and provide for their care. Others enjoyed her hospitality too.

A strongly practical woman, Ellen White stressed the

importance of simplicity, quality, and usefulness in all things. Clothing, she advised, should be durable, well-made, and also becoming to the wearer. She spoke against the practice of staying in fashion for fashion's sake. Nor did she favor making elaborate garments and complicated foods.

She encouraged uplifting reading, useful labor, character development, and Christian service instead of frivolity and purposeless activities. Stewards can be faithful in many ways.

This dedicated woman's valuable legacy to her church—a wealth of writings penned to encourage and nurture it—has guided it through many perplexities. Heeding this messenger, Adventists have prospered spiritually. Words from her pen continue to point the way to a saving relationship with the Jesus she loved and served.

PART FOUR

Personal Matters

Christian standards and ideals influence the individual's choices in personal everyday matters. These standards are guides to victorious Christian living. Ellen White wrote of their importance:

"After receiving the faith of the gospel, our first work is to seek to add virtuous and pure principles, and thus cleanse the mind and heart for the reception of true knowledge" (*Testimonies*, vol. 1, p. 552).

Nobody's Perfect, but . . . :

9 Adventist Ideals

"Whatsoever things are true, . . . honest, . . . just, . . . pure, . . . lovely, . . . of good report; if there be any virtue, and if there be any praise, think on these things" (Phil. 4:8).

Jesus' high standards affected His conduct. In following His example, His present-day disciples become like Him.

Bible Study and Prayer

To know God better each day, committed Adventist Christians pray, study His Written Word, and meditate. Some devote an hour each day to contemplating Christ's life and sacrifice. In many homes the family regularly gathers for a worship time. Together they pray, sing hymns, and study the Sabbath school lesson or other portions of God's Word.

Character Development

Adventists believe Christians must become like Jesus in thought, word, and action. Through God's power they can become loving and lovable, refined, courteous, unselfish, and genuine. Only He can give victory over every sin.

Believing that the redeemed will take only their character into the eternal life, Adventists place a high value on child training and spiritual growth.

The Bible teaches purity of speech. This rules out swearing, profanity, and vulgarity. The Ten Commandments expressly forbid using God's name carelessly or irreverently. *Gee,* a euphemism for *Jesus,* is borderline profanity. Certain other common slang expressions are corruptions of *God, Lord,* and *Jesus Christ.*

Sabbath Observance

God calls His people to worship Him on the Sabbath, the memorial of Creation (see Gen. 2:1-3 and Ex. 20:8-11). The Sabbath begins Friday at sundown. It culminates the week's work and other activities. The Sabbath ends Saturday at sundown. Adventists typically begin and end the Sabbath with a worship period.

On Friday, Adventists ready their homes and hearts for the Sabbath. They anticipate its peace and blessings. They finish their shopping and prepare the next day's food and clothing. They clean house, bathe, and shine shoes. In winter, Adventist schools, conference offices, and ABCs close early. This allows staff and students time to prepare for Sabbath too.

Sabbath is a weekly appointment with God. In preparing for it, careful Sabbathkeepers put away secular reading materials. They turn their radios and televisions off until the sacred hours have passed. Students set their weekday studies aside. Retreating from the commercialized, secular world provides time to spend with the Creator of the Sabbath. Spiritual refreshment comes from worship and fellowship. The change of pace can provide physical refreshment.

After-church activities may include sharing a meal at home, studying the Bible, going on nature walks, listening to spiritual music, and reading Christian publications. Other typical activities are visiting shut-ins, distributing literature, and conducting story hours for children.

Human Relationships

Christ set the example in all things and lived a life above reproach and without hypocrisy. Adventists believe they too must be honest, truthful, and morally upright.

The Ten Commandments, which Christ honored, outline how humans are to relate to God and each other. Obeying the commandments shows respect for the lives, rights, and property of others. Biblical principles can and should permeate all relationships and business dealings.

Marriage and Family

Adventists believe God intended marriage to be a lifelong union, with both partners committed to making the home a "little heaven upon earth." When God is the head of the family, and hearts are closely knit together, the Christian home can effectively disciple its members and help them develop Christlike characters.

Since shared ideals and goals contribute to a happy home, Adventists are counseled not to marry someone with different religious beliefs. Too often such a union produces a "home where the shadows are never lifted" (Ellen White, *Messages to Young People,* p. 440.) If an Adventist does have a non-Adventist spouse, the Adventist can do much to make his or her religion attractive to the mate. For an Adventist, only marital infidelity can be viewed as grounds for divorce.

Parenthood carries the weighty obligations of child

care and discipling. It includes nurturing the youth, guiding their character development, and training them for Christian service.

Health and Temperance

A health-conscious people, Adventists believe they should take the best possible care of their body, for it is the temple of God (1 Cor. 3:16).

Temperance includes sobriety and self-control. "It is next to an impossibility," said Ellen White, "for an intemperate person to be patient" *(My Life Today,* p. 97). Yet patience is vital to a person's Christian growth.

Adventists are taught to avoid such harmful, addictive substances as alcoholic beverages, tobacco, illegal narcotics and drugs, tea, and coffee.

"The only safe course is to touch not, taste not, handle not, tea, coffee, wines, tobacco, opium, and alcoholic drinks. The necessity for the men of this generation to call to their aid the power of the will strengthened by the grace of God, in order to withstand the temptations of Satan and resist the least indulgence of perverted appetite, is twice as great as it was several generations ago. . . . The only perfectly safe course to pursue is to stand firmly on the side of temperance, and not venture in the path of danger" (Ellen White, *Counsels on Health,* p. 125; italics supplied).

Temperance directly affects health and happiness. On a larger scale it means not carrying work, study, recreation, or even exercise to excess. Each form of intemperance causes stress on particular parts of the body. Illness and disease can follow.

In dietary matters Adventists believe food should be simple, wholesome, and natural, ample in quantity, of good quality, and taken at appropriate times. Moderation is best even in healthful foods. Overeating overloads the digestive system and makes the mind sluggish.

Country living, another Adventist ideal, offers many advantages. It can contribute to health and spirituality. The fresh air, gardening opportunities, and outdoor exercise are healthful bonuses.

Dress

"The outside appearance," Ellen White observed, "is an index to the heart" (*Testimonies,* vol. 1, p. 136). Recognizing this, Adventists recommend plain, conservative clothing rather than garments that are gaudy or heavily ornamented. Neatness, simplicity, appropriateness, and practical styles are preferred.

Adventists believe it is important for clothing to be in good taste, clean, attractive, and in becoming colors. At the same time it can be modest, properly fitting, and of good quality. This lets the wearer be comfortable and self-forgetful.

Dressing should be for health, not for show. Garments should not hamper blood flow, free breathing, or body movement. Healthful garments provide warmth and proper protection without compressing the internal organs.

Adventists usually do not wear jewelry. Adventist men have traditionally given the bride-to-be a wristwatch instead of an engagement ring. Watches worn for timekeeping purposes are not classed as jewelry.

Leisure Time Activities

The eyes and ears are gates of the mind. If, as some claim, no sensory image is ever truly forgotten, guarding these gates becomes very important. Written and artistic works, musical compositions, and dramatic presentations feed a person's mind and spirit one way or another. Some are decidedly harmful; others have little value.

Reading Material. What a person reads can stimulate or destroy interest in the things of God. That's why the Adventist ideal says to choose the good and true, uplifting, and worthwhile. Will the material read be uplifting, elevating the mind? Is it untrue? Fanciful? Vulgar? Impure? Will it make the Bible seem lifeless and dull?

Music. Some musical works are uplifting and powerful. They touch the heart and draw the listener closer to God.

Some music has a harmful effect and is inappropriate for Christians.

At home and at church, Adventists use hymns of praise and spiritual songs. They enjoy a variety of hymns familiar to Christians everywhere. The church hymnal contains these as well as hymns dealing with distinctive Adventist beliefs.

Radio, television, movies. Staying in tune with God means training the mind to dwell on spiritual themes, keeping the mind-channel open to Him. Many modern electronic media and theatrical productions obstruct this channel. Considerable care is needed in this area and others.

These influences daily bombard the senses with unchristian acts and values. Scenes of immorality and violence coupled with foul language quickly deaden the viewer's sensitivity and erode personal values. High standards are derided rather than upheld. Low standards soon appear normal, modern, acceptable. The saying "By beholding we become changed" (Ellen White, *Christ's Object Lessons,* p. 355) is still true. Thus careful selection is vital. Any entertainment that glorifies sin or ridicules Christian beliefs and values cannot be wholesome.

Recreation and entertainment. The best recreational and leisure activities will refresh and renew both mind and body. They provide a change of pace, relaxation, and perhaps a challenge. Many pleasant, profitable diversions can be found both indoors and out.

Social dancing and gambling do not measure up to the Adventist ideal.

Admittedly, nobody's perfect. Individual practices vary in the personal matters touched upon in this chapter. It is clear, however, that high ideals and standards will mark the lives of those who truly love God and serve Him.

What Do You Eat if You Don't Eat Meat?

Vegetarianism

10 "Whether therefore ye eat, or drink, or whatsoever ye do, do all to the glory of God" (1 Cor. 10:31).

Many Seventh-day Adventists choose to be vegetarians. The church encourages that vegetarianism be practiced wherever possible.

Vegetarians base their diet on plant foods (vegetables, fruit, nuts, seeds, grains) rather than on meat (red meat, fish, fowl, seafood). Generally they have no difficulty getting more than the U.S. Recommended Daily Allowance of all nutrients.

(Caution: It is unwise to make drastic dietary changes without securing adequate information first: learning how and where to obtain the necessary nutrients, and how to prepare them.)

There are three kinds of vegetarians. Total vegetarians use plant foods only; lactovegetarians use plant foods plus milk; lacto-ovovegetarians use plant foods, milk, and eggs.

As a dietary precaution, total vegetarians may supplement their diet with iron, calcium, riboflavin, and/or vitamin B-12, although this is not necessary. The use of milk and/or eggs and a variety of whole grains and green leafy vegetables provides all these nutrients. To avoid unwanted animal products (lard, for example, which is a derivative from pigs—see below), vegetarians read food labels carefully.

The Vegetarian Rationale

Of the many reasons for not eating meat, five stand out:

1. Health. Some people want to reduce their saturated fat and cholesterol level. Others wonder if animal diseases pass through meat to humans. Some question the safety of eating fish and shellfish grown in water polluted by sewage and toxic chemicals.

2. Religious. God provided Adam and Eve with plant foods to eat (Gen. 1:29 and Gen. 3:18). After the Flood He allowed the temporary use of "clean" meats (Gen. 9:1-4). Since the body is the temple of God and He wants to save the body as well as the soul (1 Thess. 5:23), Adventists seek to cooperate with Him in caring for the body He has given them.

3. Optimum land use and the world food shortage. An acre of land feeds more people when used for growing edible plant food than when used for raising meat animals.

4. Ethics. Some believe killing animals is inhumane, unnecessary, and wrong.

5. Economics. Meatless meals can be inexpensive.

Clean and Unclean

The Old Testament books of Leviticus (chap. 11) and Deuteronomy (chap. 14) list animals God specifically permitted or denied as food. Clean ones, yes. Unclean ones, forbidden. Some Bible versions read "detestable" or "abominable" instead of "unclean."

The "clean" or approved animals are those that chew a cud and have a split hoof. Therefore, God allowed humans to eat cows, sheep, and goats. He expressly forbade them to eat horses, pigs, and rabbits.

The "clean" water creatures have both fins and scales. Thus shellfish and many other sea creatures are unclean. Various birds of prey are named (eagles, owls, hawks, herons, vultures) as "unclean" and unfit to eat. Among the flying and creeping things, grasshoppers and locusts are permitted as food.

The Vegetarian Menu

But what do you eat if you don't eat meat? Actually, taking meat off the plate leaves more room for wholesome foods.

Vegetarians get essential nutrients from various foods, including:

1. Gluten, the protein part of the wheat kernel
2. Legumes, or beans. Soybeans and garbanzos rate high in protein quality. Tofu (soybean curd) is nutritious, convenient, and versatile.
3. Nuts and seeds
4. Analogs (commercial meat substitutes)
5. Complementary proteins
6. Other wholesome foods that contribute lesser amounts of protein (fruit, vegetables, whole grains). (See Table 1.)
7. Milk, which supplies adequate amounts of riboflavin (vitamin B-2) and calcium. However, since whole milk contains cholesterol and saturated fat, use mostly skim and low-fat milk and milk products.
8. Eggs. These provide high-quality protein and iron. (Caution: use no more than three egg yolks weekly, since they are high in cholesterol.)
9. Fiber. Use an abundance of whole grains, fruits, and vegetables.
10. Fruits and vegetables. Fresh fruits and vegetables contain all the other vitamins and minerals necessary for good nutrition.

What about cheese? When compared to nuts and beans, cheese is high in fat (30 percent), in calories, and in sodium. (See Table 2.) It molds readily and is easily contaminated during the cheesemaking process. Its lack of fiber encourages constipation, which gives cancer-causing substances longer contact with the digestive tract. It appears that Ellen White had good reason to warn that "cheese should never be introduced into the stomach" (*Testimonies*, vol. 2, p. 68). Some who study her writings believe she did not condemn the use of cottage cheese and fresh milk cheeses such as mozzarella.

For the greatest health benefits, food should be prepared simply.

"Fruits, grains, and vegetables, prepared in a simple way, free from spice and grease of all kinds, make, with milk or cream, the most healthful diet" (Ellen White, *Counsels on Health*, p. 115).

Companies such as Loma Linda Foods and Worthington Foods produce a wide range of meatless proteins called analogs. Based on wheat gluten, soybeans, and other vegetable protein foods, these products help meateaters ease into a vegetarian diet. Working people find them convenient, as do meateaters who prepare food for vegetarians. Adventist Book Centers and some health food stores sell these canned and frozen meat substitutes. Look for them also in the natural foods or health foods sections of supermarkets.

Can a vegetarian diet supply enough protein? Certainly. Most foods contain protein. In fact, dietitians find it challenging to devise a balanced, *low*-protein diet for kidney patients. It is easy for vegetarians to get enough protein when they eat a variety of legumes (beans, peas) and whole grains on a daily and weekly basis.

What about iron? Isn't meat necessary for getting enough iron? No. Dried beans, green and leafy vegetables, and whole grains are good sources of this mineral. Vitamin C included in the meal with cereals and grains aids its absorption. It is unwise to use tea and coffee, which reduce the amount of iron absorbed from plants.

So what do you eat if you don't eat meat? The answer—a variety of good and wholesome plant foods.

The daily recommended amount of protein is 44 grams for a woman weighing 120 pounds, and 56 grams for a 154-pound man. As shown in the table on the following page, protein from low-protein foods contributes to the total protein intake. Together these foods would supply about 43 percent of an adult woman's protein needs and 33 percent of a man's.

Table 1

Protein Content of Selected Nonmeat Foods

Food and Amount	Grams of Protein
1 cup shredded raw cabbage	1.3
1/2 cup cooked navy beans	7.8
1 cup cooked oatmeal	5.4
1 hamburger roll	2.5
4 dried apricot halves	1.0
1 small orange	1.0
Total	19.0

(Source: Charles F. Church and Helen N. Church, *Food Values of Portions Commonly Used,* twelfth ed., [Philadelphia: J. B. Lippincott, 1975].)

Getting Into the Adventist Lifestyle:

Suggestions

11 This book has shown how Adventists' beliefs influence their lifestyle. For those who want to adopt those beliefs and lifestyle, what comes next?

Find a nearby SDA church. Ask around or refer to the church listings in local newspapers. Check both "A" for "Adventist" and "S" for "Seventh-day Adventist" in the phone book. If someone gave you this book, ask that person for directions. Be persistent and get acquainted.

Attend meetings and services. Make a point of regularly attending the worship service and Sabbath school. Join a Sabbath school class and ask for a lesson quarterly. Prepare to discuss the lesson by studying it during the week. Go to the social gatherings and prayer meetings and participate.

Make friends in the SDA church. Accept invitations to Sabbath dinner. Your new friends can help you become more thoroughly acquainted with the Adventist lifestyle. Stable Adventists who have a close walk with God and live up to the church's ideals can help you the most spiritually. Be friendly, but expect some Adventists to be shy.

Follow a regular Bible study plan. Correspondence lessons, filmstrips, and videotapes are available. Group Bible studies are good ways to increase your knowledge of Scripture and make friends.

Cultivate a sense of belonging. Both before and after

baptism remind yourself, This is my family. Paint yourself into the picture.

Be a faithful Christian steward. Use your time and talents wisely for God's glory. Tithe faithfully and set aside a percentage of income for freewill offerings to projects that interest you. When shopping, make only necessary purchases. Learn to manage money carefully and cut appropriate corners.

Read. Explore the writings of Ellen White, starting with books such as *Steps to Christ, The Desire of Ages,* and *The Great Controversy.* Include other SDA authors and Adventist history in your reading too.

Most local churches have free literature available. Obtain other materials from the church library, members, and the Adventist Book Center. (Ask the publishers or the ABC for a catalog. See Appendix C for details on placing orders by telephone.)

Read also the union conference magazine as well as *Signs of the Times, Vibrant Life, Listen, Liberty,* and *Adventist Review.* The latter is the weekly bulletin board of the world church.

Tune into Adventist radio and television programs. Obtain stations and times from the newspaper and/or the television viewer's guide, or write for a station log. See Appendix C for addresses.

Get involved in helping others. Find a local church project that sparks your enthusiasm. Contact the leader and ask to be included in it. Help out with the booth at the county fair, go out with the Christmas carolers, visit shut-ins, or lend a hand at the church's Community Services center. Participate in the church's health seminars. Share what you learn and invite others to attend.

Explore Christian education. Consider its benefits. Inquire about Adventist schools that serve the area. Talk to parents whose children attend them. Ask about scholarships, other financial aid, and job opportunities. To find out what Adventist education is all about, read the book *Education,* by Ellen White.

Aim for high ideals in everything. Give the study of God's Word and a close personal relationship with Him top priority. Take time for daily personal devotions and Bible study. Pray for strength and victory, seeking God's guidance and a knowledge of His will for your life.

"While you have one desire to resist the devil, and sincerely pray, 'Deliver me from temptation,' you will have strength for your day" (Ellen White, *The Upward Look,* p. 68).

Learn how to prepare for the Sabbath and keep it. Make the Sabbath a special, enjoyable day for yourself and your family.

Maintain high standards in all areas, including reading, music, and television programs. Build a library of Christian music and enjoy it on Sabbath and other days. Deliberately choose to see and hear that which is pure and pleasing to God.

Choose wholesome companions and recreation. Attend church socials to discover SDA patterns of fun and fellowship.

Learn more about healthful living. Enjoy the outdoors and country living. Walk. Garden. Exercise regularly and sensibly. Adopt good health habits. Whether exercising, sleeping, working, or eating, practice moderation. Make only a few changes at a time.

Be open to health information from reputable sources. Reason from cause to effect, then choose the most healthful way. Learn how to prepare tasty and nutritious food. Avoid food fads and unbalanced eating habits.

Use a variety of whole grains, fruits, and vegetables, including the leafy and dark-green ones. Keep highly refined foods to a minimum. Learn to enjoy simple, wholesome foods prepared in a more natural state.

Avoid foods containing large amounts of sugar or salt, as well as pickles, irritating spices, and rich foods.

A monotonous diet increases the likelihood of nutritional deficiency, so eat a wide variety of wholesome foods. Avoid lard and other unwholesome animal products by reading food labels when shopping.

Begin the day with a good breakfast, then allow five or six hours between meals. Eat at regular times, and then only at mealtime. Discard all unhealthful recipes, replacing them with more healthful ones. All in all, eat as healthfully as possible.

Move toward vegetarianism. Start by eliminating from the diet every unclean flesh food mentioned or implied in Leviticus 11 and Deuteronomy 14. (In particular, say goodbye to lard and all forms of pork.) Remember, God doesn't ask us to give up anything that is good for us or that would make us really happy. This applies in other areas of life too.

Cut down on high-cholesterol foods. While you are learning to appreciate vegetarian protein foods, use only "clean," lean meats. Make other dietary changes slowly, thus giving the digestive system and taste buds time to adjust to the new foods.

Attend vegetarian cooking classes sponsored by the church. Have someone give you pointers in healthful cookery. For vegetarian recipes, see cookbooks such as *An Apple a Day,* volume 2; *375 Meatless Recipes* (Century 21 Cookbook), and *It's Your World Vegetarian Cookbook.* Look for these at the ABC.

Healthful eating is worth the effort. Cutting down on rich foods means fewer calories and often less weight to stress the joints. Eating fewer animal products reduces cholesterol intake as well as the incidence of flesh-borne disease. Then too, the fiber in plant foods keeps the bowels working well.

Enjoy your new lifestyle and church family. Stay with it and discover new energy, improved health, new avenues of service and joy, and peace of mind in troubled times. But most important, keep your eyes on Jesus. He's the reason for the Adventist lifestyle.

APPENDIX A

What Does That Mean?

Those SDA Idioms

The Adventist Church has developed a specialized vocabulary, using old words in new ways and coining new words to fill a need. Listed here are terms and abbreviations commonly used.

ABC—Adventist Book Center. Bookstore outlets in the United States.

Academy—Adventist high school. Some are boarding schools.

ADRA—Adventist Development and Relief Agency, International. An umbrella organization for overseeing development and relief work.

Adventist Review—Weekly magazine carrying inspirational articles and church news.

AJY—Adventist Junior Youth. For children ages 10 to 15. Usually a part of the church school curriculum. Trains for leadership and service.

Andrews—Andrews University in Berrien Springs, Michigan. Includes the SDA Theological Seminary, College of Technology, College of Arts and Sciences, and School of Graduate Studies.

Anointing the sick—A private prayer service in which elders of the church pray for and anoint one who is ill.

ASI—Adventist-Laymen's Services and Industries. An organization of professional people not employed by the denomination but strongly dedicated to witnessing and soul winning.

AYVSC—Adventist Youth Volunteer Service Corps. Encompasses all volunteer service programs of college-age SDAs worldwide.

AY—Adventist Youth. A senior youth group for ages 16 to 30. Provides fellowship and recreation, and trains youth in witnessing and leadership.

Birthday-Thank Offering—A monthly offering for missions. Expresses gratitude for life and for specific personal blessings.

Book and Bible House—Now Adventist Book Center. See ABC.

Breathe-Free Plan—Seminar to help smokers break the tobacco habit.

Brother—Man or boy in the SDA Church family.

Camp meeting—Annual spiritual gathering lasting 3 to 10 days. Sponsored by local conferences and usually held in summer for campers of all ages. Strong emphasis on successful Christian living, witnessing, and spiritual renewal.

Child dedication—Public pledge to raise one's child for God.

Christian education—Formal private schooling (usually referring to church-operated) from kindergarten to graduate school, based on Christian principles and service.

Christian Record Braille Foundation—Serves the blind and hearing-impaired by producing sound recordings and also reading materials in large print and braille.

Church Manual—A tool for church management. Outlines procedures, standards, and duties relating to local churches, members, officers, and auxiliary organizations.

Church school—Weekday SDA elementary school. Emphasizes right relationship to God and Christian service.

Colporteur—See Literature evangelist.

Company—Group of believers before it becomes a church.

Conference—Organization of local churches, usually statewide.

Conscience Project—Weekend seminars pertaining to military service and noncombatancy.

Conscientious objector—One who believes killing is wrong and refuses to bear military arms. Most Seventh-day Adventists are conscientious objectors but are willing, when drafted into military service, to serve as medics.

Dark counties—Areas having no established Adventist work or church.

Deacon—A male member elected to care for buildings and grounds and to serve during meetings. Also helps the needy poor and others.

Deaconess—A female member with duties similar to that of a deacon.

Disaster and Famine Relief Offering—Yearly offering that funds emergency aid in times of natural disasters anywhere in the world, without regard to race or religion.

Effort—Series of public evangelistic meetings.

Elder—1. A layman elected to assist the pastor in spiritual leadership. 2. An ordained minister. Adventists do not use the term *reverend*.

Faith for Today—Church-sponsored nationwide television outreach organization.

First love—Zeal and spiritual fervor of the newly converted.

Five-Day Plan to Stop Smoking—Seminar to help smokers quit tobacco use, now called the Breathe-Free Plan.

Foot washing—First part of the Communion service. Also

called the ordinance of humility.

GC—See General Conference.

General Conference—1. Administrative body of the Seventh-day Adventist world church. 2. World headquarters in Maryland. 3. Informally, the world convention, or session, of the church, held every five years.

Guide—Weekly journal for junior and earliteen age youth.

Health message—A broad term referring to all aspects of Adventist teaching concerning the optimum lifestyle.

H.M.S. Richards, Sr.—Founder and original speaker of the *Voice of Prophecy* radio program.

Home and School Fellowship—Fellowship and study group for parents, usually of school-age children.

Home Study Institute—Now called Home Study International. Nationally accredited institution that provides correspondence courses in Bible and regular academic subjects for preschool through college and adult education.

HOPE—Help Our People Evangelize. A cost-sharing plan by which conferences help fund personal local evangelism.

Humanitas—"To serve mankind." The North American Division merger of Student Missions (now Humanitas International) and Taskforce (Humanitas at Home). Youth in service to mankind for Christ.

ICPA—International Commission for the Prevention of Alcoholism and Drug Dependency. Deals with professional people and thought leaders through seminars, congresses, workshops, and institutes of scientific studies.

"In the message"—An incomplete expression that infers "a member of the SDA Church and a believer in its message."

"In the truth"—An incomplete expression that infers "a member of the SDA Church and a believer in the present truth it teaches." (See Present truth.)

Ingathering—Annual public solicitation of funds for humanitarian work. Solicitors (sometimes accompanied by Christmas carolers) offer brochures explaining the church's work and use of funds.

Insight—Weekly magazine for older teenagers.

Investiture—Awards service for Pathfinders and Adventist Youth.

Investment—An individual project to raise money for missions.

It Is Written—Television outreach organization.

JMV—Junior Missionary Volunteer. See AJY.

Junior academy—School offering grades 9 and 10.

Laodicean—State of spiritual lukewarmness or indifference; a person in that condition.

Lay activities—Christian witnessing activities by lay members. Also called personal ministries.

Layman—Church member not employed by the church as a minister.

Literature evangelist—Christian literature salesperson working door-to-door. Works on commission. Formerly called colporteur.

Loma Linda—1. University and medical school at Loma Linda, California. 2. Hospital at same location. 3. Food company producing vegetarian-type foods.

Maranatha Flights International—An organization of volunteers who donate time and skills to erect churches, schools, etc. Workers pay their own transportation and receive room and board at the job site.

Master Guide—Highest rank in Pathfinder Club or Adventist Youth. Candidates must be at least 16 and must complete specific requirements.

Message—The three angels' messages found in Revelation 14; the doctrines of the Seventh-day Adventist Church as a whole.

Message—Bimonthly publication primarily for the Black population of North America.

Mission Spotlight—Audiovisual report on SDA mission work.

Morning Watch—Morning devotions; also a daily devotional book.

Oakwood College—A Huntsville, Alabama, school serving Blacks.

Ordinances—Ordinances of the Lord's house. Consists of the Lord's Supper (Communion) and the ordinance of humility (foot washing).

Organized work—Activities of the denomination and its employees.

Pacific Press Publishing Association—SDA publishing house in Nampa, Idaho.

Pathfinder Club—Youth club for juniors and teens. Features adventures in outdoor living, crafts study, and nature exploration.

Pillars of the church—staunch, often longtime, members.

Pillars of the faith—Key doctrines of the church.

Prayer band—A small group meeting for prayer and sharing.

PREACH—Project to Reach Every Active Clergyman at Home. Sends *Ministry* magazine to clergy of other denominations.

Present truth—God's message for the last days. That is, truth for the present time, which Adventists believe to be the last days.

PRISMA—*Projeto de Integracão e Servico da Mocidade Adventista.* The South American Division's equivalent of Humanitas.

Probation—A time for deciding whether to accept or reject

God.

Quarterly—Bible lesson study guide used in Sabbath school.

Quarterly service—Lord's Supper; Communion. Held every three months. Sometimes called the "ordinances."

Quiet Hour—An independently financed Adventist radio outreach organization.

Remnant church—God's people in the last days of earth's history. A term applied to the Seventh-day Adventist Church.

Review—See *Adventist Review.*

Review and Herald Publishing Association—SDA publishing house in Hagerstown, Maryland.

Sabbath—The seventh day of the week, Saturday.

Sabbath school—Weekly Bible study and fellowship for all ages, usually held in conjunction with the worship hour.

San—See Sanitarium.

Sanctuary question—Refers to Adventist belief concerning the cleansing of the heavenly sanctuary and its implications.

Sanitarium—A medical institution providing physical therapy and other treatments.

SAWS—Forerunner of ADRA.

Self-supporting work—Christian ministries other than those officially funded by the church. Includes lifestyle reconditioning centers, schools, and vegetarian restaurants.

Series—Evangelistic meetings lasting a week or more, thus a "series" of meetings.

Signs of the Times—Outreach magazine published by the church for the general public.

Sister—Girl or woman in the SDA Church family.

Sister White—Ellen G. White, one of the SDA Church's founders.

SOS—Sustentation Overseas Service. Volunteer missionaries who are retired denominational employees.

Spirit of Prophecy—The Holy Spirit as manifested in the E. G. White writings; hence, the writings themselves.

Stewardship—The responsible use of abilities and possessions; specifically, the tithing principle.

Student missionary—Youth between 18 and 30 who volunteers a year of service at an overseas mission post. See also Humanitas.

Three angels' messages—1. God's last appeal to the world. 2. Revelation 14:6-11.

Thirteenth Sabbath—The last Saturday of the three-month cycle. Culminates a unit of Bible study and mission emphasis.

Tithe—Ten percent of income; to return a tenth to God.

Truth—The "present truth"; the doctrines of the Seventh-day Adventist Church, with particular emphasis on Revelation 14:6-12.

Uncle Arthur—Arthur Maxwell (1896-1970), author of children's books and longtime editor of *Signs of the Times*.

Unentered territory—Areas without Adventist work and believers.

Unfallen worlds—Inhabited planets untouched by sin and Satan.

Vegetarian—Person who eats no flesh foods. Lacto-ovovegetarians use milk and eggs; strict vegetarians eat no animal products.

Vegetarian-type foods—Term used in this book. Includes such items as coffee substitutes, peanut butter, meatless protein foods, and broth flavorings containing no animal products.

Vespers—A religious evening service held on either Friday or Saturday evening; usually coincides with Saturday-night sundown. .

Vibrant Life—Bimonthly magazine promoting healthful living to the general public.

Voice of Prophecy—Nationwide radiobroadcast.

Watsonville—A California warehouse for relief supplies.

Week of Prayer—A week of spiritual emphasis and renewal. Conducted once or twice yearly in Adventist churches and schools.

White, Mrs. E. G.—One of the church's founders. Also known as Ellen White and Sister White.

Witnessing—Sharing beliefs by word, action, and lifestyle.

Workers—Persons employed by the denomination, particularly pastors.

Worship—The Sabbath preaching service; also a devotional time in the morning or evening or to open or close the Sabbath.

Worthington—Ohio health food company. Makes vegetarian entrées.

APPENDIX B

Suggested Reading

Starred (*) titles are available from Adventist Book Centers.

Education

Moore, Raymond S. and Dorothy N. Moore. *Better Late Than Early*. Pleasantville, N.Y.: Reader's Digest Press, 1975. 235 pp.

______. *School Can Wait*. Provo, Utah: Brigham Young University Press, 1979. 281 pp. Evidence for delaying a child's entrance to formal schooling.

*White, Ellen G. *Education*. Mountain View, Calif.: Pacific Press Pub. Assn., 1952.

*White, Ellen G. *Fundamentals of Christian Education*. Nashville, Tenn.: Southern Pub. Assn., 1923.

Health

Cook, John. "A Church Whose Members Have Less Cancer." *Saturday Evening Post*, vol. 256, p. 40ff, March 1984.

McMillen, S. I. *None of These Diseases*. Old Tappan, N.J.: Fleming H. Revell Co., 1963, 1984. 160 pp.

*Noorbergen, Rene. *Programmed to Live*. Mountain View, Calif.: Pacific Press Pub. Assn., 1975. 104 pp.

*Robinson, Dores Eugene. *The Story of Our Health Message*. Nashville, Tenn.: Southern Publishing Assn., 1965. 445 pp.

Walton, Lewis R., Jo Ellen Walton, and John A. Scharffenberg. *How to Live Six Extra Years.* Santa Barbara, Calif.: Woodbridge Press, 1981. 117 pp. Presents vegetarianism, seven steps to health, and more.

*White, Ellen G. *Counsels on Diet and Foods.* Hagerstown, Md.: Review and Herald Pub. Assn., 1976.

______. *The Ministry of Healing.* Mountain View, Calif.: Pacific Press Pub. Assn., 1942.

Ellen G. White

*Bailey, Phyllis C. *Fascinating Facts About the Spirit of Prophecy.* Hagerstown, Md.: Review and Herald Pub. Assn., 1983. 64 pp. Various lists concerning the life and work of Ellen G. White. Answers questions frequently asked.

*Coon, Roger W. *A Gift of Light.* Hagerstown, Md.: Review and Herald Pub. Assn., 1983. 63 pp. Overview of E. G. White's call and lifework with vignettes of her mission in the SDA Church.

Gifford, Steve. *She Speaks for God.* Baltimore, Md.: Amazing Facts, Inc., n.d. 35 pp. Examines briefly a prophet's characteristics and the writings of E. G. White.

*White, Arthur L. *Ellen G. White.* Hagerstown, Md.: Review and Herald Pub. Assn.

*White, Ellen G. *Life Sketches of Ellen G. White.* Mountain View, Calif.: Pacific Press Pub. Assn., 1943.

General

**Adventist Review,* the weekly church paper.

**Church Heritage: A Course in Church History.* GC Youth Department, 89 pp. For young people studying for Master Guide or Senior Youth Leadership Certificate.

*Jewett, Dick. *Orientation for New Adventists.* Nashville, Tenn.: Southern Publishing Assn., 1978. 63 pp. Spiritual counsel for new members.

**Seventh-day Adventist Church Manual.* Rev. 1986. Outlines fundamental beliefs and operational policies for local churches.

***Seventh-day Adventist Encyclopedia*. Rev. ed. Washington, D.C.: Review and Herald Pub. Assn., 1976.

**Seventh-day Adventist Yearbook*. Annual directory of the General Conference and its divisions, union and local conferences and missions, institutions, and workers.

*Walton, Lewis R. and Herbert E. Douglass. *How to Survive the '80s*. Mountain View, Calif.: Pacific Press Pub. Assn., 1982. 108 pp.

*White, Ellen G. *Steps to Christ*. Mountain View, Calif., Pacific Press Pub. Assn., 1956.

*______. *Welfare Ministry*. Washington, D.C.: Review and Herald Pub. Assn., 1952.

APPENDIX C

Addresses

Radio and Television Station Logs

Current station logs can be obtained from the following. The starred (*) programs offer Bible and health correspondence courses.

Radio

*Quiet Hour, 630 Brookside, Redlands, CA 92373
*Voice of Prophecy, Box 55, Los Angeles, CA 90053

Television

Breath of Life, 1100 Rancho Conejo Blvd., Newbury Park, CA 91320
*Faith for Today, Box 1000, Thousand Oaks, CA 91359
*It Is Written, Box 0, Thousand Oaks, CA 91360
Search, 630 Brookside, Redlands, CA 92373

Other Addresses

ABC Mailing Service, P.O. Box 7000, Boise, ID 83707
ABC Mailing Service, P.O. Box 1119, Hagerstown, MD 21741

To place telephone orders for denominationally produced books and records, call 1-800-253-3000 in the contiguous United States and 1-800-253-3002 in Alaska and Hawaii. Give the operator your order and Visa or MasterCard number. Orders are forwarded to the ABC nearest the customer for immediate shipment.

ADRA, International (SAWS), P.O. Box 60808, Washington, D.C. 20039-9989
Adventist Adoption and Family Services
Oregon office: 6040 SE Belmont St., Portland, OR 97215

Michigan office: 125 College Ave., Box C, Berrien Springs, MI 49103

Adventist Health Network, 6840 Eastern Ave., NW., Washington, D.C. 20012

Call 1-800-253-7077 about health programs near you.

Adventist Information Ministry, Andrews University, Berrien Springs, MI 49103. A telephone answering service manned by seminary students. 1-800-253-7077

General Conference of Seventh-day Adventists, 6840 Eastern Ave., NW., Washington, D.C. 20012

Home Study International, 6940 Carroll Ave., Takoma Park, MD 20912

Humanitas, P.O. Box 5420, Takoma Park, MD 20912

Maranatha Flights International, Box A, Berrien Springs, MI 49103

Pacific Press Publishing Association, P.O. Box 7000, Boise, ID 83707

Review and Herald Publishing Association, 55 West Oak Ridge Drive, Hagerstown, MD 21740

Index

V

W